School for
My Child

School for
My Child

A little dot on the canvas of elementary schools

P R A M O D   M A I T H I L

PARTRIDGE
A Penguin Random House Company

Print information available on the last page.

To order additional copies of this book, contact
Partridge India
000 800 10062 62
orders.india@partridgepublishing.com

www.partridgepublishing.com/india

Foreword

My curiosity about "School For My Child" was aroused when I read the name of the school Anand Niketan DEMOCRATIC School (ANDS). After all, most schools are not democratic. The time table is rigid. The curriculum is determined and teachers have very little space to demonstrate and practice freedom and democracy. There is a small experiment one can do to check if you have freedom in your classroom: simply walk out into the halls and go to another room. If chaos ensues then it means that you have been ruling your children. I have taught in classrooms where there have been 40 children and only 12 children. Of course it is easier to have a democratic classroom with less children but if the classroom is large enough, one can also have groups and stations for 40 children where they pursue their own activities and discussions. Yes, the classroom will be louder, but students can still learn to direct a certain amount of their own activities and learning. ANDS is now at the point where they have to decide for reasons of financial stability, whether to become more conventional or find funding to continue the present pattern.

Pramod, his friends and supportive parents have proven that even small children can learn to discuss matters, debate issues and reach decisions in a responsible manner. Children have learned that their voice is important. More than that, they understand that everyone has a voice and needs to be heard. We often talk about "respect". This word has different meanings for different people. Respect is often determined by one's wealth, social status and position of power. These young children are learning that respect must accrue to all peoples and that they also must demand respect for themselves.

It would be fascinating to watch the progress of these children into adulthood. My personal findings would testify that children who have actively participated in their own learning are certainly more proactive, and co-operative. They have better communication skills and have greater confidence. They show more care, concern and compassion for others and for nature. Children, who have learned from an early age to discuss and debate, also come to an understanding that there are myriad patterns and connections in society, the natural world, and academics.

There is a "thermostatic principal" proposed by the late social scientist Neil Postman. It states that when it is too hot the thermostat needs to be set down. When it is too cold, we need to warm up. The present assessment system treats children as merely numbers; there is no place to study our relationship with the natural world, text books are the be-all and end-all, hands-on activities are only reserved for a half hour art class once a week. Free play needs much more research and understanding. Obviously the thermostat needs some adjustment.

This sincere effort will give everyone food for thought. We will look forward to the next book three years from now.

Ruth Rastogi, Teacher and Pedagogue

From the author

I'm not a writer by nature or preference. So book writing isn't my cup of tea. Nevertheless, I have attempted to author the book you are now holding, which moves away from some of your ideas of a normal book. In it, I share my experiences in learning and education in the hope that others will find a useful perspective on many issues in learning and education. Whether professional, researcher, parent, educationist, teacher, student, or someone reading for pleasure, I hope all of you find something useful and interesting.

This book takes you through the exciting journey of the evolution of the Anand Niketan Democratic School (ANDS) in Bhopal, of which I am one of the founders. I have also been the Director of the school since its inception. The book primarily documents my learning and work during the initial three years of the school. At times, the two journeys, mine and the school's, have diverged, even to the point of collapse. But there has also been a meshing of ideas and approaches that are distinct from the norm. I hope this story will serve as a reference point for those who wish to start an innovative school of their own. For reasons of individual comfort and sensitivity, I have not used the original names of some of the players in this collective learning experience.

English is not my first language so I admit the rather unrefined written text of my first draft was edited by my friends. I've attempted to write the book in a 'talk' format, hence you might find slip-ups and repetition at places. It's a collage of ideas, practices and reflections, which, I believe, communicates ideas sufficiently well in my personal style and tone. We are all gradually transformed by our life experiences so I hope the write-up truly describes the ups and down, positives and negatives of this personal evolutionary journey that has been constantly shaped by circumstances and experiences. It is important to note that due to the language editing processes at places the text may reflect that I have made well-planned decision but actually in most cases it emerges from. Such as grouping emerges as need as young children do not stay longer for any activity due to their attention span and skill sets. So started calling them Butterfly. Age was easy to recognize them.

I have tried to trace this gradual unravelling of my own experiences from the initial understanding to a certain degree of maturity. In some instances, unsuccessful episodes may have created obstacles to the flow, but I chose to include them in detail as an important part of the evolution. But a selection that leaves out some episodes is also necessary to remain within the readable text limit decided for the book. I also acknowledge that certain links are hazy in my memory so you may find some narratives abrupt and jumpy.

I have chosen to write this book because current circumstances are worrying for the school, forcing it to dilute the radical path it's been progressing along till today.

The school was established against the flow of mainstream educational thinking and such initiatives take time to self sustain. ANDS finds itself in a similar predicament. The school team has decided to change some of its approaches so it can achieve financial sustainability faster. I remain a dissenting voice. I'm convinced ANDS will never be the same it was in last three years. That's why I felt this compelling urge to document its journey till now.

This book distils the knowledge I have gained from my readings and the cross-pollination of ideas in my interactions with colleagues, friends, family, children and visitors to ANDS over the years. They all deserve credit for whatever a reader might find valuable in this book. As for all that is less than valuable, I own full responsibility as the author.

The following pointers indicate how the contents of the book have been organized.

- The book begins with some highlights and experiences to make the reader curious about ANDS.
- The second chapter is about thought processes and the theoretical journey of ideas before the school started.
- Chapter 3 is a detailed tour of the school that traces the evolution of various activities and other elements.
- In chapter 4, I share my experiences in language education, which was originally published as an independent article on how children learn language.

- In chapter 5, I have presented perspectives on mathematics education at ANDS.
- Chapter 6 is, again, an independent article on the assessment system we have evolved at ANDS.
- Chapter 7 is a collage of different thinking and practices at ANDS and outlines some of my dreams and aspirations.

I dedicate this book to my parents, Badri Prasad Maithil and Phoolwati Maithil, who have been my inspiration all through my life.

I gratefully acknowledge my friend and well-wisher Rex D'rozario and Ruth Rastogi for their time and expertise to proof and edit the language of full book. A special thank to Amit (children at ANDS call him Ben10), who went through the text and gave suggestions. I especially thank Dr Ashwin Kotnis, Archana Zulfiqar, Dr Arvind Gupte, Adil Ahsan, Avinav Kumar, Kapil Bajaj, Rustam and Teji who reviewed chapters to improve the language.

Special recognition goes to Prakriti, my daughter, Abeer, the three-year-old son of my colleague Vijay & Kavita, and all the other children at ANDS. They are the primary source of my learning.

I am grateful to Kamal Mangal, Chairmen of the Anand Niketan Group of schools, whose trust in me and financial support brought ANDS into being. I have learnt a lot from his long experience in running and managing schools. I am also thankful to the advisory members of the ANDS team: Rajesh Khindri, Tultul Biswas, Dr Bhavesh Shah, Grishma

Shah and Namita Jha. My discussions with them on the school continue to refine my understanding.

I thank the school team for their valuable contributions in running ANDS and helping me along in this journey of learning. They include Vijay Jhopate, Stephney D'vas, Satish Bhasker, Namita Bhagat, Anil Singh, Varsha, Nidhi Solanki, Shikha Banskar, Ankit Singh, Shobha Natarajan, Annora, Pooja Bajaj, Devi ji, Vinod and Santosh. I also thank Rajni Mehta for encouraging me to write this book.

My wife Namita deserves my heartiest thanks for playing several roles in the writing of this book. As an art teacher and core team member of ANDS, she has helped me clarify many of the issues we have faced. Her day-to-day support and encouragement as my life partner has been invaluable in completing this project – when I got stuck somewhere her presence lightened the atmosphere.

Contents

Some highlights of the ANDS experience

After visiting Anand Niketan Democratic School (ANDS) in Bhopal, a student of education wrote back to us:

> *"Concluding my comments on my visit to ANAND NIKETAN, I can say that a bright ray of hope is seen in the bold initiative taken to create a better kind of education for children and it gives me a picture of children becoming promising social and political citizens. I give my warm wishes to the school to prosper and create an ideal model to be followed by the rest of education system."*

Several such comments and words of appreciation encouraged us. However, my joy and motivation comes primarily from real-life experiences with children. So before going into details of the idea behind ANDS and its functioning, I wish to share with my readers some exciting snippets and observations about some of our ANDS children that reflect their personal journey to joyful and participative learning:

Apramey come out of his shell

Janhvi visited our school one day, eagerly having a look around. I knew her because she is Apramey's neighbour. I gave her a guided tour of the school and a brief overview of how its various features flow from our understanding of learning and education. Janhvi listened with interest to all I had to say, expressed her good wishes for our effort, and then explained what made her curious about our school.

Apramey, she said, was a shy and diffident child – before he came to ANDS. He would usually stand behind his mother, holding the edge of her kameez, not feeling confident to face unfamiliar people, let alone mix or play with them. The boy spoke little, just nodding his head shyly in response to friendly overtures.

"Do you want to play, Apramey?" Janhvi would ask him, only to receive a nodded 'no'.

"Should I go, then?"

Again a nod, with not a word spoken, signifying, "Do so, if you wish."

Then, within a matter of weeks, a dramatic transformation occurred in Apramey's behaviour. Within three months of schooling at ANDS the 'shrinking violet' had turned into a confident and communicative child, Janhvi observed.

"I heard him loudly singing '*Ik din bik jayega maati ke mol*'. And the other day he confronted a much older boy to get his ball back. That was not the Apramey I knew. The change was quite dramatic," she said.

Not surprising, therefore, that she was curious to know what went on in a school that was having such a transformative influence on the boy.

Apramey's parents told us he was earlier in a 'conventional' or 'mainstream' school. They would receive complaints about him: "It's difficult to make Apramey do anything in school."

But the boy actively interacted with his parents.

It's a usual characteristic of conventional schools to govern a student's behaviour with strict Do's and Don'ts: 'Don't look outside', 'Don't talk', 'Sit quietly', and so on. I have reasons to believe this school environment turned Apramey into a shy and diffident boy. A child in such an environment feels everything he or she does is judged as appropriate or not appropriate, while an adult seems to have all the privileges. Maybe that's why most children want to grow old faster.

Apramey was shy when he joined us, but was full of spirit and spontaneity like any normal child. He showed that spirit in ANDS' free and trusting environment, not taking long to overcome his diffidence and grow friendlier with people around him.

He started off as a silent observer of the school routine and learning activities. Then slowly, he began to talk about his favourite 'action heroes' - and everyone listened to him attentively. I'd like to imagine that Apramey was encouraged when his personal interests received a respectful space in the school. He has since continued to share his feelings with us and grown in confidence.

It's gratifying to see he's now fully enjoying his childhood. Learning seems a lot more fun to him. It's no less fun for us to see we have been able to provide an environment that frees our pupils from restrictions they don't need. That's what produces the sometimes dramatic outcome Janhvi spoke about.

Parth leaps for joy!

The following is an English translation of what a parent of an ANDS pupil posted on his Facebook page along with this photograph:

> *"The boy on the 'tyre trolley' is my friend and son – Parth. He's been going to ANDS for the past 7-8 months. The trolley running on rails is part of an innovative learning environment featuring thematic classrooms and democratic functioning that the school has created to foster self-learning. Earlier, Parth had studied in class 1 and 2 in a mainstream school. I think he must have attended classes only for a few months during that time. I never pushed him to go to school every day. He never talked about his school. He didn't even know the names of his friends. If a stranger appeared before him he would retreat into a shell like a tortoise. Even if a familiar face came home he would start crying. This same Parth cannot wait to go to school now. He sings unselfconsciously before an audience. Ten days ago he played the role of Daku Angulimal in a play 'Gautam Buddha' staged in school. The startling change I have seen in my son is a remarkable statement of what 'true' education can achieve.*

Watching Parth playing Daku Angulimal brought tears to his mother's eyes as she heard the loudest-ever voice of her 8-year-old son.

Parth was the third child enrolled in ANDS after we opened for admissions. He was a quiet and diffident boy but didn't take long to open up. Within a couple of weeks, he had become more observant and began taking part in school activities.

But suddenly, at one of our morning assemblies, Parth began jumping up and down, singing loudly and off-key. This went on for a day or two before he calmed down and became more balanced. It was rather funny, but it also made me think. This was probably the first time Parth had experienced a free environment at school and he wanted to exercise/enjoy the freedom. Let me admit that I was little worried initially that 'where this is leading to'. But I do not want to give my judgement on his act as authority. He might have found that working with hand, interacting gently, making friendship etc are rather productive. And also he might have received a massage from his colleagues that it is lathering to them. It's certainly reason enough for the kind of joy Parth expressed and returned to a balanced way of living.

Such boosts in a child's confidence were some of the significant and encouraging outcomes we observed in all ANDS's pupils. No child looked forward to the end of the school-day when they had to return home. Our van driver had to round them up. Parents told us there was no hassle in sending their children to school in the morning; they went willing and were ready to go!

I never liked the image of children making a dash for the school exit at the very first ring of the closing bell – like prisoners finding an escape route. It reflects something negative about the school - as if children are hemmed in physically and mentally.

I have not designed things keeping this/certain outcomes in mind. All the outcomes are 'by product' of everything happening at ANDS. What makes ANDS different is its freer environment where adults take care not to assume the role of a figure of authority nor be perceived as one.

So how is this environment compatible with education and learning? Let me try to answer the question in a metaphorical way.

Let's assume we want a child to learn to climb a ladder. Most conventional learning methods detail how the child should lift her/his leg and put it on the first step. We may also design an activity to balance on one leg.

Provided a ladder, young children always tempted to climb if not I would suggest creating something which motivate her to climb up the ladder (you may place a flower up there or so). She would then try different ways to reach the top of the ladder. In the process, she learns to climb the ladder on her own. An adult could be around to help, if needed. The adult may even climb the ladder, to excite and show the child how it's done. The point is, learning to climb a ladder is not objective for the child but the child wants to go up this learning is just a **by-product** of all his/her efforts. Once she masters the skill the child uses it in different situations to reach newer heights. She enjoys her success. Interestingly, while experimenting with different methods she may even discover her own unique way of climbing the ladder. So there could be lots of variations in the discoveries of a group of children.

At ANDS, the role of the adult is to organize resources and work equally along with the children, exposing children to different dimensions of different areas of enquiry being explored and the ways to learn.

ANDS gives equal value to all the skills, content and knowledge in different areas of learning. Art and craft are not merely 'extra-curricular' activity but given as much importance as, say, language and math. What's important is to preserve and nurture the inherent inclination of children to art and craft. ANDS succeeded in this. If you visit the homes of our students, you are likely to find their works of art and craft adorning the drawing room.

Prakriti settles for a 'brand' of creativity

One day, my daughter Prakriti, now an 8-year-old, asked me for a bottle of 'Mirinda', a fizzy, orange-flavoured drink. The grocery store I visited had no 'Mirinda' so I brought her a bottle of 'Fanta' instead. That's another brand of the orange-flavoured drink. But she refused to take it. I was a little surprised. Prakriti likes fizzy, cold drinks but I had no clue she was becoming so brand conscious! Next day, I bought her the 'right' brand. However, it was not until she revealed her attempt to make a toy out of a 'Mirinda' bottle that I learnt that it wasn't brand consciousness but something else going on inside her head.

I tried to trace the sequence of events. She had found the head of a broken doll somewhere and wanted make its body. She probably recollected that a 'Mirinda' bottle was just the right shape she needed for the missing body – like a woman's torso, with the swell below the neck forming the chest, a taper in the middle resembling a shapely waist and a cylindrical bottom hidden by the fall of a long skirt. She visualised fixing the head into the bottle with a little decoration and making a doll to play with. So with a bit of help from me, she fixed the head into the bottle, stuck two hands made of paper rolls and covered the body with paper, finally colouring it in colours she liked.

Other examples of core academics are often visible in children outside school.

Satakshi discovers a method of keeping accounts!

Saurabh related this anecdote about his six-year-old daughter Satakshi at a parent-teacher meeting. The father and daughter decided she would receive Rs5 daily to save up and buy something she wanted. The arrangement worked fine for some time. But then Saurabh would skip a few payments due to his busy work schedule and make the payments in bulk a few days later. Satakshi couldn't keep track of how many days were missed and whether she had got the total payment due to her. So she drew a grid on her notebook and ticked off the days she received payments. This simple tally accounting that she had developed on her own and shared with Saurabh solved her problem of keeping track of payments.

Bihu's initiative brings a wall newspaper to the school

A cartoon series featuring the popular character Doremon inspired Bihu, our 8-year-old pupil, to start a newsletter on her own She told us she got the idea while watching a character in the series taking a picture of his friend and printing it on paper. She immediately switched the TV off, went to her father and told him she wanted to publish a newspaper of her own! And she did, manage to bring out three weekly editions all by herself.

Other children then got interested and joined her in starting a common wall paper for the school. After a lot of discussion, they decided to call it 'Ullu Bullu Bacche'. It is basically a display board that brings together news, write-ups, pictures, art, etc 'filed' by our reader-reporters. We believe the wall paper will have a positive effect on the children's familiarity with the written word.

Such initiatives are not beyond a child's ability but they are uncommon. Why aren't all children so creative and enterprising? To answer the question, we need to cast a critical eye on the system of education in our schools.

The Aprameys, Parths, Prakritis, Satakshis and Bihus make me excited to describe ANDS, the school in which they study. ANDS is an attempt to create an alternative model for education at the elementary school level that is pedagogically a self-learning process steeped in democratic and inclusive values.

ANDS comes into being

Several people, working in the field of education dream of a school that embodies their ideas of what education ought to be. I dreamed such a dream when I was working with Eklavya, an NGO conducting field-based research and implementing a science education programme in middle school education and teacher training. The dream came true with the setting up of ANDS. Anand Niketan Democratic School (ANDS) is an attempt of this Natural Learning Environment by organizing resources, design contextual activities which motivate children to experiment with the skill and information and the democratic education to achieve inclusion in schools. ANDS made a successful attempt to create a pedagogical alternative for education at elementary level which I would like to name "Natural Learning Model". The school completed three years of operation in 2014.

This chapter is a sharing of how the idea of ANDS was conceived and how it has evolved. My pathfinder guides were the contemporary discourse on education, the available literature on education and pedagogical research, and policy documents such as the National Curriculum Framework of 2005 (NCF 2005) and the Right to Education Act of 2009 (RTE 2009). I began to get a better understanding of the theories I studied when I actually started working on the basis of my broad, personal insights. Over time, I traced the threads of theory emerging from practice. They helped me comprehend the situation better and move ahead. This chapter outlines the observations and anecdotes that helped me relearn and improvise my theoretical understanding.

Looking back, I find my understanding of learning and education developed in two streams: (a) an appreciation of concepts/theories and (b) insights into the 'system' of education. The two aspects overlap and advanced simultaneously. (a) is concerned chiefly with *what education is* and (b) has more do with *how education should be organized*. I'll try to give a flavour of each of these two aspects.

The journey of developing ANDS
Content vs Process

I first confronted the problems of education after I began working with Eklavya in 1998-99 in its Hoshangabad Science Teaching Programme (HSTP), which was an effort, begun in 1972, to reinvent and enliven the teaching of science in schools run by the government of Madhya Pradesh state. Some of the problems of education that affected my understanding are listed below:

- First, schools overemphasize information i.e. memorizing 'facts', an approach rooted in the widely held misconception that knowledge is factual information.
- Second, the examination system has constrained the achievement of our educational objectives, if well-rounded learning and development is what we set out to achieve. Today, the edifice of education is constructed around examinations.
- Third, non-academic activities are given secondary status, at best, or looked down upon, at worst. Manual work, sports and activities that express our emotions and imagination are often absent from school practice.

While working for the HSTP, I realized the syllabus and subject-matter should be no more than a means to facilitate the development of the child into a thinking and understanding person.

At ANDS, we changed our focus from subject matter/ information to process i.e. the *how* of education. Learning by doing, discussion, reasoning, creativity, shared/cooperative learning, and democratic norms of conduct are the essential elements of our pedagogy. Education is not a mere textual exercise. Children spend a lot of time in playing, living friendship, art, craft, gardening, exploring their relation with the environment, singing and acting as part of their daily routine.

For example, every child has a tree friend in school they talk to and play with. They hug their tree clean the area around and water it. They collect stories about their tree and write poetry about it. They observe living beings that seek shelter in their tree, and are wary about its leaves being damaged, looking for the reasons for such damage. They share their observations and efforts with the other children. This activity leads to new, open-ended learnings. They go on to explore the morphology of plants, their sensitivity to the environment and so on.

Assessment proceeds with the academic and non-academic processes, without disturbing the child's self learning journey.

How do children learn?
"Children learn through anything and everything"

The work I was doing with the HSTP, interspersed with some reading, gave me a foundational understanding of how children learn. I subsequently built on that understanding, but a basic insight had already emerged: If this is how children learn, here is how their education should to be organized. In other words, the system of education should correspond, as closely and faithfully as possible, with our understanding of how learning actually takes place.

Children have an uncanny ability to grasp and learn. The ways in which they learn are more varied and complex than we imagine. Let me take an example of a five-year-old child who learns his mother tongue. How does the child learn the language? He does not know it when he is born yet we keep talking to the child. He must feel like he's being bombarded with different sounds and responses. The child manages to comprehend and very soon starts picking up the language.

If adults need to perform a similar task of extracting sounds and associated responses out of a collection, they classify and categorise the sounds with their different and correlated responses. They then need to have a program to pick out the sound and its associated response. Children do all this with no help from adults and start communicating meaningfully by the time they are three years old. We hear countless examples of sentences/words they speak without any adult speaking these sentences/words to them. Parents don't teach them the sequence of alphabets or simple sentences. The children learn all this and more themselves. They understand without being taught, which recalls Plato's problem: How is it that a child knows so much given so little? This holds true across the world's languages.

In later years in school, the 'mistakes' children make may suggest how much they have understood or what else is needed to consolidate their understanding of a concept.

Just try to remember your reaction when your child spoke her first word. You did not care how precisely she spoke i.e. you ignored the 'mistakes', instead hugging her in sharing your excitement at her achievement. This gives her the signal that she is going in right direction so she continues her attempts and learns the mother tongue as a result. We do just the opposite in schools by unconsciously humiliating children by pointing out their mistakes instead of responding positively to their achievements.

So what do these insights into learning tell us? We should ensure that we create a holistic environment to let the child explore. At ANDS, we give young children every possible opportunity to express themselves and we respond sensitively to every attempt they make. We create the ground for children to observe, question, experience, articulate, act, make 'mistakes' and develop their own understanding.

For example, an eight-year-old child decided to produce a newspaper, titling it '*Chandni* अकबार' (Chandni newspaper). There was small error in writing the name – अकबार (*Akbaar*) instead of अखबार (*Akhbaar*). No one bothered about the mistake but appreciated her effort, pasting it on the school soft board for others to have a look. She must have watched some of her friends reading the word exactly as it was written because she later corrected it in even finer script with the Arabic notation (*nukhta*) under the ख (*kh*) (अख़बार).

Let us take another example, One day a 6-year-old boy came running to office and said '*Hamko kaamyadi mil gayee*'. (We succeeded). There was a small mismatch in his pronunciation. The teacher responded '*Tumhe kisme kaamyabi mili?*' (What did you succeed in). He used the correct word '*kaamyabi*' whereas the child had said '*kaamyadi*'. The child responded '*Keel nikalne mein*' (In removing the nail). The teacher did not point out his mistake but joined in his excitement, giving the child the opportunity to hear the correct word. Such responses help children to realise their 'mistakes' and correct them while also impressing upon them the need to improve their language and communication.

The argument of the 'lump of clay'

We often hear children being likened to a blank slate or lump of clay, which the teacher and education are supposed to write on or give shape to.

Various contemporary educational discourses, the NCF 2005 played an important role in correcting this misconception and pointing out that children enter school with a storehouse of previously acquired knowledge. Every new experience is a process of interaction with this previous knowledge to form new knowledge, the process being influenced by their social environment.

A better metaphor would be to liken a child to a seed with all the potential to grow. We need only to nurture the seed by creating the proper environment around it. Let's take the seed metaphor a step further: a mango tree cannot grow from an apple seed. The implication here is that while seeds require the proper environment to grow, each seed is unique. So each child is unique and learns in her/his own unique way.

If a child's learning is built on previous knowledge, we don't have to start from scratch – the blank slate. At ANDS, we have created an open-ended environment and activities that children can join in. Some activities are developed by the children themselves. Perhaps the idea can be better understood with a activity of maths room: the facilitator and children have created a bazaar of shops and a centre to exchange ANDS money (specially developed currency for education) among themselves. The children already know about money transactions and the various shops around them. Using this knowledge, they create their own world together.

Why is there a division of subjects?

I was thrilled when I first learnt this argument in a workshop. The NCF 2005 elaborates it in a focus group paper that talks about the parameters and basis of different knowledge categories. I would like to share the logic behind categorising three areas of enquiry discussed in the workshop - mathematics, natural sciences and social studies.

Let us examine the basis on which these subjects are divided. The first column of the table below contains three statements. The second column contains the parameters/ methods to test/verify whether these statements are true. After discussion, the key elements in differentiating between the three statements were noted in the third column.

No.	The statements	Parameters/methods of testing the truth	Key element
1	2+2=5	Required facts which are predefined (axioms) & logical analysis	Axioms
2	X bird lays eggs in summer	Definition of 'X' bird and 'egg', observation & logical analysis	Observation & controlled experiment
3	There shouldn't be reservations at all	Definition of terms, survey, opinion collection & logical analysis	Human/social Interest

The completed table indicates the differences in the nature of the three subjects.

Mathematics: We have a few fixed definitions known as axioms which are abstract constructs that do not exist in reality. The study of mathematics is built on logical deduction/induction starting from these axioms. That is why mathematics can be very precise and absolute, its conclusions being overarching, with no exceptions. That is why we study content in mathematics established years back.

In the given example, the meaning of the symbols 2, +, = and 5 are absolute so there is no doubt about the statement, unless we change the meaning of the symbols. I'll give another example to elaborate. If we need to prove the sum of the internal angles of a triangle is 180 degrees we don't ask children to draw triangles and measure their internal angles to discover their sum is 180 degrees. This method has two limitations from a mathematical perspective:

1. Whatever scale we use, we cannot get an exact measurement, the answer varying because of the least count of the scale. So it is possible we may not get 180 degrees as the sum of the three angles.

2. Drawing a mathematical triangle on paper is not possible. In mathematics, a line has zero thickness. We cannot draw a zero thickness line so a mathematical triangle cannot be drawn on paper. What we draw is actually a model of the triangle.

Suppose we ignore these limitations and use the method to prove the theorem. We can measure the internal angles of a limited number of triangles and add them for individual triangles. Say we measure the angles of 100 triangles. We can make the statement about those 100 triangles but we cannot be sure about the same result for 101th triangle. In the study of mathematics we use theoretical deduction or induction to establish the result for all possible mathematical triangles.

Natural sciences: We study our natural environment and the objects and life forms that exist in it. We ask questions about natural phenomena, observe them and try to locate cause-and-effect relationships between them to see if a pattern emerges.

In the life sciences statement in the table, we first need to define 'X' bird, egg, summer and the process of laying an egg. Then we observe and note if a certain number of 'X' birds laid eggs in summer. We can then generalize that 'X' bird lays eggs in summer. If we find 1-2 examples that deviate from this observation, we add them as 'exceptions'. If the number of exceptions increases, we modify the statement. We may conclude that 'X' bird with a certain specialty lays egg in summer, or make some other new observation. Statements in natural science should be stated with conditions. We have to be ready to accept the exceptions and change the theory.

In the physical sciences, we define various objects and conditions. We then observe or devise an experiment in which we try to create all conditions same except 'one factor'. Later, we conclude the change occurs because of the 'one factor'. Various such observations and patterns are then assembled into a generalized theory to explain any phenomenon, which is subject to change/reformulation with new observations and experiments. For example, observations of the movement of the sun and earth earlier led to the explanation 'the sun moves around the earth'. This explanation changed over time with new observations and experiments to 'the earth moves around the sun'. You never know tomorrow somebody may come up with a better explanation.

Social sciences: We deal with humans and society with all their interests, value systems, relationships and so on in the social sciences. Interpretations could change from person to person. For example, if we conduct a survey to find out if there should be reservations or not we do not get a single or unique response. But to proceed in decision-making the group would choose a suitable response based on its values and concerns. Nothing reaches the level of absolute truth in the social sciences.

We thus have a fair picture of the basic differences in the nature of content in different areas of enquiry. I believe we require different states of mind (mood) to study or work on content in these different areas. The conventional school does not acknowledge this. One subject teacher enters the classroom immediately after the other subject teacher leaves at the end of the period. It gives no space for children to switch their state of mind (mood) for the next subject. I believe it would be difficult for any child to keep switching his/her mood for every such short period of study time throughout the day.

To express this in simpler terms, I would like to share a small example. I had found an interesting book on probability so I carried it along with a couple of other books to read while I was travelling. I took the book out to read but then started reading a story in a magazine I had picked up instead. I thought I'd go back to probability after that. The story was so touching I just couldn't focus on probability after I finished reading it. I found it difficult to switch moods immediately.

I'm sure many of you may have had similar experiences in your life. We have countless examples of teachers complaining about children looking out of the window and day dreaming, not taking any interest in the subject being taught. The reason is not always what's being taught is uninteresting or pitched high/bellow. The school set up does not give a student the space to build up interest. That's why teachers in conventional schools have to spend so much time in managing the class. 'Listen carefully', 'Concentrate on what you're doing', 'Don't disturb others', they keep shouting in an annoyed voice.

Every intellectual and non-intellectual stream of work or enquiry requires a certain mood for study or activity.

The ANDS design makes this switching smooth for the child. The teachers (facilitators) sit in different rooms and the children move to these rooms after every learning session. Unlike the conventional setting, there are no grade-wise classes; instead, we have thematic rooms - Room for language and enquiry, Room for numeracy and logic, Room for art and aesthetics and so on. It becomes easier for a child to switch to different states of mind (moods). If children are listening to a story in the language room, they have enough of 'buffer' time to disconnect after the story ends and then connect with the facilitator, activity, materials and ambience of the next room and begin a new learning experience with a different theme that they themselves had selected in their pre-planned schedule for the day.

The social science research perspective

My learning in this area gave me a radical view of education. In the natural sciences, inanimate objects behave in the same way if the energy and method applied to them is the same. One can control most of the factors and the objects do not have a say in the process. For example, if I wish to throw a stone to a particular spot, I can meticulously plan my strategy, calculating the distance, the force required, and other factors and throw the stone to the spot, achieving my objective. This cannot happen in education. Just assume a bird in place of the stone in the above situation. Many factors then cannot be controlled. Most important, the bird is a living being. We should not forget that in education we are dealing with children, who have their self and their interests. The whole idea of pre-planned steps in a fixed sequence to achieve a uniform result cannot apply to education. The planning has to be different, keeping in mind the child is an active agent and has a stake in whatever is happening in a learning process.

This approach to education has influenced the ANDS design. The school is full of resources for different areas of inquiry. We discuss and propose activities for the children and they make a choice or suggest modifications. We don't focus on how these activities will shape the children but allow them to proceed according to their interest and pace, documenting their work making observations about them and taking note of interesting anecdotes in their interactions with the subject of enquiry and their peers. We try to trace the pattern of learning and growth. Based on this data, we re-organize resources and modify activities to enrich their exposure and fulfil their needs.

We keep in mind the aspirations of parents and of the nation while organizing the resources and environment. Every day at the end of school the facilitators sit together and discuss what's happened in the different thematic areas. This helps us prepare for the next day. We keep track of the progress of each child and modify activities and content, dropping ideas that don't seem to work.

For example, the number activity for a group of 10 children using matchstick bundles for addition is a popular game-activity in most schools following activity-based learning. Children throw dice and collect matchsticks to the value shown by the dice. The one, who collects the maximum number of matchsticks and bundles is the winner. The game did not appeal to children at ANDS after they played it twice. So next day I went with an interesting board game involving addition.

It's not a factory

Reading *Danger School*[2] helped me connect the dots and realize our schools are modelled on the factory system, with children being treated as inanimate raw material to be processed into finished products. The influence of mass production techniques is unmistakable in the grading of children by age, standardised textbooks, the same methodologies and assessments. It's intuitive to realize this model is ill-founded to the point of being abusive. There is no correspondence between an industrial process leading to the manufacture of a product and the process we call education. The latter deals with human beings in all their social and psychological complexity. So we need to take a second look at our school system and make some fundamental changes.

At ANDS there is no fixed sequence for the teaching-learning process or the content. We have full faith in the children and believe that if they are allowed to do things at their own pace and interest in an atmosphere of stimulation and thoughtful guidance, they can learn to their optimum potential.

As a democratic school we do not impose any sequence of activities for any group of children. We have designated thematic areas with motivating surroundings and all the required resources for children to undertake a range of activities to develop their capabilities, acquire skills and even choose a way of life. The themes of the different areas are based on our understanding of children's learning as well as the aspirations of parents and the nation. Assessment for the children is continuous and comprehensive and assessment techniques keep evolving. The developments/changes in each child are registered and shared as feedback with all stakeholders.

At ANDS children's age were not central criteria to divide them in to groups but gradually the groups start emerging based on their level of understanding and skill sets. So you will find children of different ages in the thematic rooms at any given point. The groups are fluid as children switch groups for some specific activity. Instead of a single textbook we have located a variety of resources and every room has its library. Children are not assessed by uniform criteria - we get a different story about each child. I will discuss these aspects in detail in other chapters.

Mirror of social disparities

I have visited around 500-to-600 schools in Madhya Pradesh. I believe the school system is designed to reproduce and mirror the social characteristics and values of our society, such as authoritarianism and stratification based on income and wealth.

The school system is also a vital means of perpetuating social disparities and classes. There are schools for the wealthy, schools for the middle classes and schools for the low-income groups. The reality is that schools come at different 'price points', making for an ever-finer stratification of society. These stratified/stratifying schools have their own aims and outlook with little concern for those they deem below their class. Even in a conventional, government-run school, which is said to be free of such market forces, the classroom dynamics perpetuate social disparities.

So our schools reinforce social exclusion and alienation. They are also seen as de-motivating, alienating and repelling children. The children who are successfully 'schooled' become perpetuators of social disparities rather than the change agents one would like them to be.

The RTE Act 2009 advocates inclusive education. ANDS is structured to implement this concept in actual practice. Students participate and claim ownership of the school irrespective of their economic background, caste, creed, gender or attainment levels. At ANDS we did our level best that every student, including the differently-abled, gets equal opportunity to explore the world around, live in a community, participate in decision-making and become active self-learners.

Authoritarian system

Teachers are widely accepted as a figure of authority both in terms of knowledge and discipline. Seen as the 'official' repository of knowledge, they are conditioned to become the 'rightful' enforcers of propriety and rectitude in the life of students. 'Don't argue', 'be quiet', 'don't move', 'move in a queue' and other such pre-emptory instructions are their tools of enforcement. Children learn to follow their orders and rarely dare to think or do anything different, even if they feel what they're doing isn't right or proper.

At ANDS, children can choose to visit different thematic rooms every day. Their choice is based on the suggestions of the facilitator or their own suggestions for the room activity. They have a platform to share their feedback about specific activities. Asking questions about everything they see and do is normal practice in ANDS. You will not find the facilitator managing the children. Rather, they participate in the activity organized in the thematic room. Adults don't interfere in what children are doing unless they are asked for. Any intervention is only to make the children aware of the possible logical/natural consequences of the step they are taking. If adults suggest a step they present the logic behind the suggestion.

The teacher

By and large, people tend to blame the teachers if schools are unsuccessful. Teachers are also unhappy and de-motivated. I would like to present it differently.

I had been visiting a village school near Hoshangabad to work with children on mathematics. One day, a teacher from the school showed me a huge collection of handmade teaching-learning materials lying in a box. He told me when he joined the school he was also enthusiastic, he had prepared and used these materials. He did so for many years. He has spent 22 years in the school. Now he is not as excited about all this material and has stopped using them. I was speechless. But I understood the different factors that must have affected him - monotony, working in isolation, no support system, large quantum of work, low position in the education hierarchy, and so on.

At ANDS we ensure that the faculty embarks on a learning journey along with the children. Teachers share their experiences and attempts with their peer group during the feedback meetings. They do not feel isolated. They are seen as researchers and innovators of new activities to meet the children's learning needs.

I admit that being human we do have ups and down mood due to our social and psychological surroundings. I do not claim to be always ideal but learn from our mistakes. We worked towards developing and strengthening systems as means to **review and reflect**.

People do a lot of work at their work places (schools) and gather a number of experiences of innovative and creative practices. Because of lack of appreciation and feedback, these gradually taper down over the years. Many informal spaces already exist in the school. We put efforts to enriching those spaces for informal **sharing and** continuous learning by **feedback** from colleagues.

My experiments before ANDS

I would like to share this brief write-up of my experiments and experiences in schools and learning corners before I ventured to set up ANDS.

A learning space for the natural sciences (tinkering) – After the HSTP was shut down in 2002, we at Eklavya were struggling to create a space for field experiments and research in education and disseminating our ideas. This was the time I decided to work further on my school idea by joining an existing school to learn how schools function and implement some of my ideas about classroom practices. I joined Sahtyadri, a school run by the Krishnamurti Foundation of India, as teacher of science and mathematics in the primary classes. That was in 2006. I was good at making models and designing simple experiments. So, apart from my regular (and, I think, innovative) work in the classroom, I built a huge two-metre periscope, produced hydrogen in an injection bottle, made a multi-nail chair and conducted various other interesting experiments, shared these with the children in morning assembly.

Children came to know about my interest in doing and designing small, interesting experiments and models. One child came to me and said he wanted to produce hydrogen gas in an injection bottle. We performed the experiment together. This created an impetus among the children and they gradually started coming to me. I had found an empty room and managed to set up a small science room with some simple tools/equipment and odds and ends the children had collected from their surroundings. This became a space for children where they could build models and perform experiments. The room was a collection of children's ideas and dreams. That was its biggest asset; we called it a junior lab.

To kick start its functioning, I helped the children make some simple scientific equipment - kaleidoscope, periscope, pin-hole camera, lens-hole camera and so on. Many of those who took interest and participated in this activity were known to be weak in academics. When children used to come to me with an idea I simply encouraged them to attempt to make it, providing support, if required. One child picked up a pipe lying in the playground and made periscope out of It with little help. Interestingly, he was one of the students who was 'weak' in studies, according to the other teachers. Other students also began exploring ideas, like making a kaleidoscope out of glass strips, which led to making big and small kaleidoscopes and even kaleidoscopes with more than three glass strips. We ended up with 10-to-15 different versions of kaleidoscopes. This was my first successful attempt to actualise the thematic learning space idea.

Learning space with puzzles and toy display – I came back from Sahyadri and re-joined Eklavya in 2008. This time I worked on mathematics education. Shortly into my second tenure with the organization I once again got the chance to create a learning space. I had started visiting a school to observe how children learn mathematics, which later got converted into a small action-research project. Halfway through my research, the school asked me to discontinue the project since they needed time to cover the syllabus. By then I had become very friendly with the children so I negotiated with the village heads to let me use a room outside the school gate that was locked and unused. I collected books, building blocks, toys, tangrams and other puzzles and materials.

The children helped me set up the room, sweeping it and organizing the material. They brought clay-toys, matchbox toys, wooden carts and other toys they had made at home, finding the room the best place to display them to their friends. They started coming to this learning space before school started. This was also a successful experience. But I had to abruptly close it because almost half the school started coming and it became hard to manage the numbers. Also, the school allowed me back into the classroom. This experience also gave me useful insights into the possibilities of different types of learning spaces and 'sharing' as important motivational force.

A pre-school setup – I decided to shift to Bhopal in 2010. While trying to take my dream school project from the drawing board to something more concrete, I found myself looking for another school that I hoped against hope would be 'good' enough for my four-year-old daughter Prakriti. I was joined in this daunting search by the parents of two other children - Isha (Grishma-Bhavesh) and Ambar (Tultul-Rajesh). We were in the same boat, sharing the same critique of 'mainstream' schools and looking for something that corresponded to our conceptual framework, not something that was readily available.

As it happens in such situations, we eventually settled on a compromise. We found Mom2Mom, a private pre-school, and persuaded the management to start an 'independent class' that would free children from competitive pressures and give them a space to be with a community of similar age-group children learning according to the own interests and pace.

The Mom2Mom school owner was the mother of one of my students at Sahyadri and I suppose this made her develop the confidence to allow us to start the separate class. We named it 'Ninad'. She said if we could convince 7-8 parents to join Ninad she would be willing to take care of the expenses of this initiative (i.e. appoint a teacher, material costs and place). We succeeded in convincing 8-to-10 parents to admit their children to a class where children explore nature, interact with each other, listen to stories, act in plays and so on.

This time we were a team. We converted the Ninad space into a text-rich environment with poems, rhyme posters and characters from storybooks. We followed a thematic approach to learning, preparing the content and conducting the sessions with a facilitator. We timed the themes according to seasonal and other variations to maximize the linkage between real-life experiences and classroom learning. So rain and water was covered in the monsoon months, vegetables were taken up in winter when a large variety is available in the market. Children actually visited the grocery to buy vegetables as part of their classroom activity. Skills like counting, speaking, listening, reading, pre-writing and pre-number concepts were interwoven in the activities on an everyday basis. This was another learning space exploration, this time a group of like-minded friends had also been formed.

Effectively, my experiments were in three types of learning spaces - for natural sciences, mathematics and language.

I was able to evolve my understanding of approaches to learning in these disciplines through these experiences. Along with my continuing readings and discourses with friends, these learnings helped build up a strong base. My mind was stimulated enough to contemplate drawing up a plan for a 'better' school. I prepared a conceptual framework for my kind of school and shared it with friends in informal discussions, which helped me improve the idea.

So the idea of this school evolved out of my years of exploration in education and schooling. There were no particularly good or outstanding experiences from my own schooling that contributed to this, although there were no significant bad experiences either. I cannot locate exactly when the idea of this dream school began emerging but I do remember that I started putting things down on paper around 6-7 years back, especially the experiences I felt would help me give shape to the dream.

The green signal for ANDS – The Ninad classroom lasted a year. We realized the intervention would not be smooth and sustained unless some of us actually become part of the school decision-making team. That's when we started exploring the possibility of setting up our own school based on the learnings evolving in my mind. When we thought of bringing the initiative to life, one of the major issues we faced was financial. We had been interacting with Kamal Mangal, the person who had set up the Anand Niketan chain of schools in Gujarat, for Ninad and other educational matters. He agreed to help us.

Let me share how this turning moment in my life came about. Rajesh was in Ahmedabad for some personal reasons. I suggested he can spare some time for a meeting with Mr Mr Mangal and request for. Fortunately he also agreed. I went to Ahmedabad and I along with Rajesh met Mr Mangal. The meeting went on for an hour during which we shared our vision and dream. I found Mr Mangal, who is well informed about education projects around the world had also been thinking along the same lines. He promptly agreed to help us in setting up a school in Bhopal.

It was a huge challenge to translate those ideas on the ground. I left Eklavya in mid-September, taking full responsibility for executing the plan and running the school. Mr Mangal, Grishma-Bhavesh, Tultul-Rajesh and Namita-Pramod (myself) became members of the 'Advisory group' that would provide inputs guiding the course we took.

How ANDS got its name – While developing the idea, I had initially decided to call it 'The Parallel School' since its design emerged from the critique of conventional schools and education. I saw it as being 'parallel' to conventional schools. As the details of the framework for this new concept began falling into place, I felt a better name would be 'The Concept School'. I also considered 'Natural School' since it was to develop an environment suited to the 'natural' learning style of children.

When the idea crystallised well, I used the term 'Alternative School' while sharing the concept with Mr Mangal. At this stage it had become a joint venture of professionals working in the field of education. We decided not to register the school as a separate organization but to function under the umbrella of the Anand Niketan chain of schools. Mr Kamal also insisted on the Anand Niketan label. We explored a few more names before deciding to add a tagline and name the school Anand Niketan – a Democratic School.

Choosing the term 'democratic' was a way of signifying the children's stake in the educational process and also the norms for adult functioning. It was appealing - adding an elegant touch – and also communicated practice. But it differed from the 'democratic' schools around the world, most of them in developed countries, where it seems okay even if children learn to read when they are 15 years old. You wouldn't find parents in a country like India having the courage to accept such. We had to keep parental aspirations in mind. So for me the term signified that our school was an exploration to develop an Indian version of a democratic education model.

The school is now known in Bhopal by its abbreviated form ANDS (Anand Niketan Democratic School). The name makes us strive more in the direction of becoming a truly democratic school, a process in which parents are also participating. What began as a one-person initiative has grown in three years to become a cooperative effort run by a team of people.

Concluding remark – It is difficult for me to articulate in detail my understanding of education in relation to the ANDS idea. Broadly, I would say there are three aspects of the ANDS practices.

1. Nature of content, its hierarchy and co-relation.

2. How children learn?

3. Methodology, which includes classroom practice, school environment etc.

Other features of ANDS include democratic functioning among children, between children and adult facilitators, and among adult facilitators, active participation of parents, and constant evolution of learning and other processes.

But we are now at a crossroads. After three years, we find that sustaining an experimental school like ANDS and making it self-sufficient in terms of financial resources is a long journey whose direction we do not know. We have been receiving financial support to take our experiment forward but external funding will end in a year or two. The school team is now discussing how to negotiate future financial support or what needs to be done if such support is no longer easily forthcoming. Can we survive if this quantum of outside support stops or is reduced? Would we have to modify our approach to education and heed the voices of some of our parents to move closer to the mainstream to become more in tune with market demands for a kind of education that focuses on success in the job market? Would that attract more students and help us to work towards self-sufficiency?

These are questions we are asking ourselves. They are difficult questions because it would mean diluting the ideas we set out with on this exciting journey in school education and even sacrificing some of our objectives of leading children on a path of critical self-discovery and self-learning in which they acquire democratic and inclusive values to become caring human beings. It's also the reason why I think I need to jot down our experiences and learnings before the direction of our journey changes.

A tour of ANDS

With everything in place, including finance and a support group of people working in education, ANDS came into being – fulfilling our vision that was in the making for 7-8 years. I left Eklavya in mid-September 2011 to hunt for a campus for the school. We found a residential building in a newly developed area of Bhopal to locate the school. It was large enough to meet our needs and had a sizeable open area for children to play in. We wanted the school to look like a home.

The school building (design to control): Schools are designed to suit the teaching-learning method they use and organize their resources accordingly. Teaching a text is the central concern of conventional mainstream schools so they are designed for this purpose. The desks in classrooms are designed to seat the children in rows facing the blackboard. They sit the whole day in the same posture on specially designed desks with inclined top only for reading and writing. The classrooms are also usually in a row, with a corridor outside and a central room for the administrators to keep an eye on the school activities. They have one or two doors opening into the corridor, the back door usually kept closed. The toilets, laboratory, library, play area and kitchen are located some distance from the classrooms, ensuring the children can visit these areas only at scheduled times.

A home, on the other hand, is rather personalized design, with spaces and materials organized for the purpose they serve. For example, there are rooms and furniture for dining, relaxing, studying and sleeping. We need to rework this design to move away from the narrow view of education as textual learning to the view that education is a comprehensive set of academics, values, skills and attitudes.

The bungalow I found for our school was built for residential purposes. It wasn't palatial but had enough spaces for children to engage in activities comfortably. We signed a rent agreement in mid-September and decided not to make any structural changes but to redesign it into a resource-rich learning centre that looked and felt more like a home.

Spaces outside the building: To make the best use of the building and open space in the premises I researched a couple of sources, including a book 'Buildings as Learning Aids (BALA)' by Kabir Vajpeyi, and prepared a list of changes to be made. They included a uneven shaped small splash pool, and around 300sq ft of space for a kitchen garden and compost pit (which we never got down to digging). I came up with some novel ideas to make playground equipment out of trash. We made a swing-cum-merry-go-round out of a truck tyre cut in half and hung with four chains attached to a bearing at the top. A truck tyre hung between two poles became a standing see-saw. The most creative idea was to make a trolley, which became a hit among the children. The 'track' was made using two 30ft pipes with a stopper at both ends. Two jeep tyres placed one atop the other on four wheels became the trolley.

I know children love to play in the sand so we created a 150sq ft sand-bed. There were also two small lawns where children could run, hop, skip or play kabaddi. The campus had many trees such as mango, amla, pipal, paras pipal, false ashok, lemon, guava, katahal, chiku and a variety of palm. There were also shrubs like tulsi, arhar and pomegranate as well as a profusion of flowering plants - rose, marigold, bougainvillea, hibiscus etc. We decided to maintain all these and also plant touch-me-nots and a few more varieties of flowering plants that attract butterflies. I knew that the water and greenery would attract birds and other creatures, give the children ample opportunities to observe nature.

The rooms: – The bungalow had seven rooms, a large hall, kitchen, four bathrooms and connecting passages. I redecorated and refurnished the rooms to make them more engaging and comfortable for children. I removed the auto-shutting doors also put the door handle down since young children find it difficult to pull them open, placed small wooden stools in all the bathrooms so children could reach the washbasins and taps without help or difficulty. I fitted a couple of green/white boards in every room and oil painted the walls of three rooms in green up to a height of three feet for the children and teachers to scribble on. I also put up 2-3 soft boards and small racks for children to display their drawings and models and placed open wooden racks in all the rooms for storage space.

Sharing and display can be a good source of motivation so to encourage children to display their work – drawings, paintings, write-ups etc – Namita suggested a design of open photo frames, which one side wooden edge was not fixed so the children could easily change the drawings. I also disconnected all electric sockets of lower height and kept a big LED television in the main hall for their audio-visual needs.

Initially, we felt there was no need for an administration/principal's room. But once the school started functioning, we realized we needed a space for interacting with visitors, preparing worksheets and documents and doing other administrative work. We assigned a corner with a telephone, computer and wi-fi. The 'corner' now occupies a bit more space in the main hall. Anyone can use this space – it is not assigned to any one person. We sit wherever convenient with visitors and parents. There is still no principal's cabin and all spaces are open to the children. They can ask us to vacate the corner if they want to use it or the hall. We may have to allot more space for school administrative work but I would still like it to be within the reach of children. We also began with the idea that all tables and chairs should be of a child friendly height and size but we had to make a concession and get some adult-height furniture because parents and visitors did not always feel comfortable sitting on low chairs.

The children: We spread the word about the innovative school we were setting up. We started with five children, the first admissions being our own children, and the number slowly grew to 12 but again fell when five children were withdrawn. The reason for the withdrawal was that parents found it difficult to tread the unconventional path even though they agreed children should learn according to their interest and pace. They saw their children developing in different directions and not following the conventional milestones such as learning the alphabets in scheduled time by schools and not being given homework. Nor were children divided into grade-wise groups. These practices disturbed them so they put their children back into mainstream schools, even if it meant paying much higher fees.

But what they refused to see was that their children liked going to ANDS and went willingly without the usual morning hassles of getting ready for school. Their oral language skills improved dramatically even if they did not know the alphabets and they were becoming confident learners. It took us time to address the concerns of parents but we gradually managed to come up with innovative solutions without compromising our core philosophy, which I shall discuss later.

In the second year, we found parents who were well informed about progressive educational initiatives around the world were admitting their children to ANDS. Word-of-mouth publicity saw the friends and acquaintances of these parents admitting their children in the third year, with the student population growing to 28. All this happened without any planned marketing strategy or propaganda neither because none of us had any expertise in marketing nor could we afford to seek such professional help.

As mentioned before, we began by not dividing the children by age into grade-wise groups. We had two groups in the first year – young children and older children. But we soon realized we could not function with such a wide age span because the children in these two broad groupings were at different stages and levels of learning.

So in the second year, we split them into three groups - Butterflies (aged 3-4 years), Birds (aged 4-6 years) and Squirrels (aged above 6 years). But when the Squirrel group saw children moving to the next level in the third year we limit the age of the group at 6-8 years and added a new group Rabbits (aged 8-10 years). You must have noticed that we have used age here as the children's skill set match with the age group. We have also used conventional name for parents to relate with outside world.

However, the groups were not of one year limit but different group children with skills matching or interest in the day activity were free to join the group of choice for the relevant activities. For example Yatharth was just 6+ years old but he had learnt to read and write at home and in his earlier school. So he joined the Rabbits at the podium and in some other activities. However, he decided not to join the social science classes since his language reference points were yet to develop to that level.

The basis for segregating the children into these groups is explained below:

Butterflies (age range 3-4 years parallel to Nursery) – These children have developed basic motor skills and adult-like body proportions, allowing them a greater opportunity to explore the world. Initially, they still feel a little insecure in the outside world, sometimes few even crying to go back to the familiar comfort of their homes. They gradually become more at ease and love spending time playing with blocks, with friends and on the swing or in the sand and water outside. They like playing with colour and writing on the board with chalk. Their attention span is minimal and they keep switching from one activity to another. Their energy level is high if they feel comfortable in school.

Birds (age range 4-6 years parallel to KG 1&2) – 'Play age' is an unspecific designation given to this age-group. The children are active and ready to explore the world in their own ways but they are choosy at this stage. However, they do spend a good amount of time with others in organized, joyful activities. Their attention span is still evolving; they can stay a little longer than Butterflies in meaningful activities. They enjoy being with friends, start questioning and begin to understand that they have feelings and opinions that are different from others.

Squirrels (age range 6-8 years parallel to Grade 1&2) – Children are now ready to explore the academic world and learn. They look to the facilitator to suggest activities they can choose from and plan their day with little prompting on the green board. Six-year-olds are not yet ready to accept failure/defeat, but become more realistic later. I remember when Prakriti was around six year old, she would never let me beat her counter in board games where as she liked to beat mine.

They are curious, creative and sensitive. They remember activities they started better than when they were younger and do work they like with more rigour. It is relatively easy for them to understand the logic of an activity being suggested to them. This is the time they acquire basic reading and writing skills in languages (their home language or mother tongue, usually Hindi, and additional exposure to English) and numeracy.

Rabbits (age range 8-10 years parallel to Grade 3-to-5) – Children in this group now turn into independent learners so they choose to work on their selected task and ask for help only if needed. They plan their schedule in a diary given to them. Their world view is now expanding. They are expected to have a preliminary grasp of reading at least one language and elementary understanding of numbers up to 100. They are now able to read the time on a watch.

A day at ANDS

Flaxi Timing Idea: Children who use the school bus facility arrive by 9.00 am. We have introduced flexible timings so there are children who come before or after the opening time of the school day. This means there is no adult standing to inspect what time the children arrive or to scold latecomers. Children can come late. Because of various reasons we have to make a schedule for the school to start and end. It may not always match with children's choice. Our endeavour is to make the morning activity exciting enough for children to be eager to join in time. Those who come early spend their time playing on the swings and other outdoor equipment in the playground. Most children are in school by 9-to-9:10 am. Sometimes, some of them drift in only by 10.00 am but if this trend continues, we talk to the child and her/his parents to figure out the reason and see if we can pitch in.

Creating exercise: At 9.00am, a facilitator, calls the children together for some physical exercises. They gather in a rough circle so everyone can see one another. A single circle is enough at present because the total number of children is low. As their number increases we will have multiple circles. There is no fixed exercise but everyone does some running/jumping/body movements to loosen the body and ease stiffness before the school activities begin.

Picture what happens during an exercise session. When the children gather, the Facilitator declares Parth will lead the exercises. Parth stands silent, unsure about what he should do. The facilitator prompts: "See, Parth's hands are stretching out, let's all do the same." The children stretch their hands. The facilitator then asks Parth: "What's the next step?" Parth bends. So do the children. Then he straightens up and jumps. The children follow suit. That's how the exercise develops and is completed. Then Prakriti suggests a new exercise – cycling and jumping. The children cycle and jump. Sometimes the facilitator prompts the children to do more conventional exercises.

Refreshing start of the day with songs: Most of the children arrive before the exercise session is over. It's then time for singing. We go to the multipurpose hall and sit together, singing songs in the morning gathering, which is usually conducted by Varsha. This is another point of difference from conventional schools where children usually sing patriotic songs or religious hymns, with one or two chosen to lead the singing. The morning songs are great fun. The singing is loud but the children are melodious and the 20-minute session adds an air of freshness, giving a lovely start to the day's school journey.

We have a collection of around 50-to-60 songs and their number keeps growing. The children choose the song they want to sing, which include folk songs from across the country, such as the Kumaon *'Bedu pako bara masa'*, Bengali *'Ekla cholo re'*, Jharkand *'A budhau gaye chale ek, shipo shipo gadha diyaa renk'*, UP *'Ugh dina'*, Tamil *'Chinne chinne ashe'* and many others in different languages - Marathi, Hindi, English etc. There are songs covering themes like the soil, air, water, light and love as well as popular children's songs like '*Nani teri morni*' and '*Aha tamatar bada mazedar*'. Anil plays the *dhapli* (tambourine) to accompany the singing.

Singing is a space for children's creativity. They move with the *taal* of the song and act out the lyrics. They also play with the songs, adding interesting variations. For example, if there is a hen in a song, a child would cluck like a hen. Rhymes with 3-4 stanzas would be extended to 10-15 stanzas with their own creations, like '*Machli jal ki hai rani*' gets additions such as '*Tave pe dalo pak jayegi*' or '*Bahar phenko sad jayegi*'.

School announcements time: We had no space in the school to share information on issues of common concern. We recently introduced this announcement time to share information about the day's logistics, which children need to know to plan their schedule - which facilitators are available for the day, which activities are not possible on that day and so on. It is not a regular but needs-based feature. Schools tend to impose systems that become rigid and fixed.

Podium: a platform for oral expression

After the morning gathering you'll hear the children announcing its 'podium time'. This is an important feature of ANDS so I'll describe it in some detail in this narrative.

The podium is a daily hour-long session during which the children and facilitators sit together to reflect on what they had done the day before. It is an individual activity, enhanced by group feedback, in which each child takes turns to speak about the previous day's activities, with the facilitators also choosing to speak sometimes. The facilitators write down whatever the children says in each one's podium notebook, which later becomes one of the important sources of data for assessing each child's progress.

How the podium developed: I'll tell the story from the time of the first podium even though the podium today has no direct connection with it. I just want to share the process of how this activity emerged from those initial random attempts.

In the early days, children often commented there's no study in our school, we only play and have fun. I was surprised that they did not recognize the academic value of various activities in the school. Their perception of study was typically based on reading and writing and math skills.

I decided to bring out their perception about study. I conducted a discussion in which they pointed out positive differences between ANDS and other conventional schools. Their perception shifted from 'no study' to '*khel khel mein* study' (learning through play), but still not much study. We then performed skits about a day's teaching and suggested the children also develop similar skits based on their perception of schools. I did not find it significant there, the next step I thought of was to get the children to share the day's activities from a 'podium' and we, as faculty, would point out the academic aspects of the activities they had done. The children started but we could not continue our part as the 'Podium' was communicating the education aspects of the activities they did. That's how the podium activity started. It led to children now saying we do study. But I do not give credit to this evolving perception to the podium alone.

Some thoughts on the podium: Let me share some of my observations about the podium:

> The kind of things children sometimes mention during podium time are things we never took seriously or thought were 'important'. For example, one day a visitor to the school attended the class briefly for a few seconds and left. The next day many children mentioned her participation.

> Sometimes they talk about incidents happening outside the school. For example, one day the van driver made them wait for some time in the van because of some technical fault in the vehicle.

> We understood the strength of this activity when, one day, the children quite clearly said they did not like the numeracy class yesterday, forcing the facilitator to think again and look for different methods to introduce numeracy concepts to children.

> This is an interesting platform to exercise the skill of 'economy of thought'. Many things happen on a day which they feel should be taken up in the next day's podium but they learn to discriminate between what is important and what is not and select only those things worth sharing with the

group. When they speak the general pattern is to start by saying, '*Kal mai aaya tha, morning gathering kiyaa. Fir Podium kiyaa tha. Fir planning kiyaa, fir pahalee ganit ki class huii....*' (I came yesterday and did the morning gathering, after that we did podium, then we did planning for the day. This was followed by our math class.... so on. We see a gradual but significant improvement in their oral articulation and language. As they grow older they start sharing 'to the point' experiences. Gradually they change to something like 'I came did routine thing then went for our math room'.

➤ This is also a space in which we recognize a boost in oral articulation of individual the children. I would like to underline that these were not pre-decided objectives of podium.

- Reflective speaking – one child who initially merely reported the previous day's activities now reflects about these activities, giving reasons why each activity was done and what the children think about it. For example, Amber would say I did Numeracy activity but I have to do it in rush as there was another very interesting activity just after that.

- Expressive speaking – another child who also started by merely reporting activities now presents the details in an expressive way that has her audience listening to her with full attention and enjoying her presentations. Prakriti may widen her eyes and hand to tell about huge things and shrink herself to talk about an ant. She also modulates her voice when needed.

- Organization of thought – one day, Bihu started her report saying: I will be talking about three things on the topic. First is about x, second is about y and third is about z. so here is the first….. I was surprised and happy to see the way she had organized her thoughts before speaking.

- Coherence – There is gradual and significant improvement in this. I would share about a stark different in a child who was reported mild weak child whose mental age, many said, was not equal to his physical age. He initially spoke in short, unconnected sentences, that too after much prompting from the facilitators. He now reports the activities fairly fluently, in proper sequence, often expressing why he likes the activity.

- Confidence – Many children who initially dreaded speaking on the podium gradually gained confidence and some of them now speak fluently.

➢ We also came to know that three children could not pronounce a few alphabets in their day-to-day language (such as *'ada'*, which is *'ra'* with a *nuktha)*. We realized this alphabet is not part of the dialect they spoke at home. I had no issue with language with more or less specific sounds. But the additional common sound may give batter status to these children. We acted couple of times as if we didn't understand what they were saying, and some children genuinely asked for a clarification, which made it clear to them something was missing in the way they communicated. The children understood and with little careful observation and experimentation two of them have filled in the gap to a extent.

➤ It works two ways. This is a place where the children also learn new words from different dialects, such as '*mundi*' for head and '*kane*' for near.

The podium today: The podium has evolved as the number of children increased. Now each group of children plan their day differently as detailed below:

Butterflies: After the morning gathering, you will see children of this group gathered around the facilitator, who interacts with them and prompts them to share. They have a number of reasons that motivate them for this activity. They all want to sit on the hot seat to speak. Sometimes, they measure their speech with the length of written feedback in their note book. I would like to share one interesting experience. Ananya once said she did not much like an activity she was doing and expressed her dislike by holding up two closed fingers. But she enjoyed the next activity and showed her pleasure by holding up the two fingers, but this time opened wide. Apparently, the facilitator, unable to put in words the child's expression, had earlier drawn the fingers in these two positions in her notebook to denote dislike and joy. They may not sit still but they listen carefully, adding or responding when required and they felt participating in podium of her friends.

Birds and squirrels: The children are a little more organized at this age and do not need to be prompted to speak. The two groups conduct their podium separately but I have clubbed them together here because the process is more or less similar. They have institutionalized the process. Couple of things became a ritual to formalize the hot seat or podium stage, attentively listen with detail as audience if they find the speech interesting. The children usually clash over who will speak first. We attempted many strategies to sort this out - random selection, first-come first-speak, rhyme counting; pointing to the next speaker, voting and so on. Initially, they also tend not to listen to others who are speaking but then slowly begin to take an interest. A very fast improvement in their oral language is significantly visible among children of this group.

Rabbits: This group is now able to read and write, so they start writing what they will say and share with each other. Some children from the squirrels' group who know to write also join the rabbits' podium. They have different methods of sharing their reports. Sometimes they exchange notebooks and read aloud, sometimes the facilitator reads for them. At other times they read aloud their own reports. One child writes her report at home and shares it in school because she finds there is not enough time to write during the podium activity. A few children attempt to write in English and some use the Roman script to write in Hindi. I strongly believe similar development in their written language would emerge ahead as we saw in their oral language.

After the podium, the children plan their day's work in different theme rooms. Before discussing the planning and thematic rooms let me tell you a few things about the ANDS design.

The ANDS design

I was clear that if we change the core design of the conventional school, we had to review and rework each and every thing. We decided to break the mould, such as the provision of 'classrooms' according to grades, with teachers arriving to 'take' their periods with little or no resources. Instead of 'classrooms', we set up learning centres as 'theme rooms' for Language and Enquiry, Numeracy and Logic, Art and Aesthetics (Visual and Performing Arts), Child Scientist, and Sense of History and Society, Space for physical activities and Health in addition to multipurpose hall, garden, kitchen etc.

These theme spaces are equipped with materials according to the field of enquiry, and have a facilitator with expertise in that particular field. In this design, the children move across the rooms, not the teacher (facilitator). The design confers many benefits and opportunities, which we discuss a little later in this chapter. These rooms organize and facilitate activities and support learning in the particular arena which may occur in environment of the child.

Children plan their day

The biggest advantage of this design is that the children now have the option to decide where to go first. They plan what they want to do for the day and choose which theme-room they wish to go to and when. This arrangement is driven by their interest and initiative, unlike in conventional schools where the system decides what students will do. People usually ask whether this disrupts 'discipline'. I say discipline is important but it should be self-driven, not externally imposed. At ANDS, children visualize their day's schedule based on their interest, mood and logistics, which they share with the school. The school reorganizes itself in order to meet their suggested schedule. Children practice 'self-discipline' by firmly following their schedule they propose.

This effectively means we do not have a pre-decided time-table but a schedule of visits to different theme rooms worked out by children every day. They could decide not to do numeracy in first session but choose to continue the water filter activity in the EVS room first. They can also ask us to change whatever we have planned in the room if it is not engaging enough. But we do ask them to make some changes in their schedule according to our logistics and time commitments to other groups, which the children respect, so they rework their plan.

Nowadays, the older groups claim they are falling short of time and cannot plan everything they want to do on a particular day. We keep track of their schedule to ensure the proper exposure. We also place conditions - for example, that they should plan one language or numeracy session for a certain period of time. They can always negotiate with the facilitator to create attention-grabbing activities. From day one, the last period is scheduled as play time. Earlier, it was called 'do-as-you-please' time with or without a facilitator but is now called play time.

We have always been firm that the children should stick to their plan because we have also scheduled and organized our time according to their planning. The premise is articulated as 'one should respect other's time as well'. Except for a few incidents over the last three years, we never had the opportunity to exercise 'firmness'. Children agreed with the argument and change their schedule only if they have compelling reasons to do so.

Evolution of daily planning: The first time we asked children what they wanted to do. They asked for whatever we can offer. We gave them suggestions from which they could choose a schedule of activities. The first day they chose all the activities in the sequence we suggested.

They soon realized there were some activities they did not like much and wanted to leave. We were a bit firm with them at this point because we had one facilitator who spared the time for them. Although, we never forced anyone to be in the room if they did not like the activity. Instead, we encouraged them to argue against the activity and suggest replacing it with another of their liking, pointing out they had the full right to do so.

The children then began asking the facilitator what exactly they would be doing in a suggested activity before planning the schedule, becoming more careful in their planning in the process.

I would like to share an incident of their negotiations in planning. One group once had only four children who were planning their day. They had a dispute among themselves. One child wanted to do numeracy first because the math facilitator had to leave at 1 o'clock while the other three suggested doing language first because they were in the middle of an interesting story started yesterday which they wanted to complete. I commented that we could conduct a class for one child but it would be better if all together chose which room to move into. The argument went back and forth, with the one child first agreeing with the other three and then the three agreeing with the lone child. Eventually they decided to go to the numeracy room first. The thumb rule is that the majority wins but sometimes the rule doesn't hold good.

Initially, the children would write their suggestions on paper and hand them over to us. Then we started using the board, with suggestions drawn in balloons or clouds. But we would end up planning the schedule in tabular form on the board. This planning system has remained stable, although as the number of children increased, different groups made their plans independently. We now discuss the planning process in each group in detail. But I must add here that if anyone wants to initiate the planning process in their school, they should let the system evolve because anything imposed may not work.

Butterflies: Their day plan is fairly flexible. We propose and organize activities for them depending on their mood and interest. The children do not stress much on learning textual things but they aspire to make their life meaningful in school. As a result they develop their self-confidence, preserve their innate abilities and learn to the fullest of their potential.

Birds: The day plan does not make much sense to them either but we expose them to self-planning, formally declaring a schedule made by incorporating their choices. We organize activities to respond to their questions and needs. Our interest is to let them explore the world, egged on by their curiosity and hold on oral language, asking questions and using the tools and resources at their disposal to look for answers. We are also interested in letting them develop and re-inforce their language skills and readiness (mother tongue, with exposure to English). In developing their understanding of pre-number concepts we also try to give them some initial exposure to symbolic language as a strong tool in learning.

Squirrels: – This group starts to independently plan its day on the scheduling board in the main hall during which they write their names and choose the activities from the suggestions given. Sometimes they themselves suggest activities for their group. At this age they are learning to read and write and do not know how to read time on a watch, so we have a set time for different sessions throughout the day and draw a watch giving the time on the scheduling board for every period, also mentioning the duration. They do not make a fuss about which activity to go to first but around 4-5 months later they begin arguing among themselves about the schedule and choices. We insist they should be firm in observing their schedule.

Rabbits: They can all read and write and also tell the time. This group plans its day in its schedule diary. The children still plan according to the suggested time division but we expect them to extend/reduce the time according to their choice of work in future. They negotiate and argue a lot in planning their day's schedule, their reasons being multifarious. Let me share an example of a scheduling dispute:

B: *"Aaj Anil sir ki class karenge."* (We will ask Anil sir to take the class today.)

P: *Nahin, dukaan dukaan hi khelenge."* (No, we will continue the 'shopping mall' activity)

BH: *"Kya roz roz jod ghata hi karte rahenge? Kuchh naya karte hain."* (Do you want to keep doing 'plus-minus' every day? Let's do something new.)

One child insisted on working with a particular facilitator whereas others were interested in continuing the previous shopping activity while one child wanted to start something new. The dispute became heated, with everyone raising their voices and one child even crying. They finally settled on a consensus schedule without adult intervention. But there are sometimes sub-groups in Rabbits doing different things though that's not usual because, I suppose, they do want to work together.

Here's another noteworthy development among children regarding planning. I once overheard them, arguing about why they need three periods for drama. One said we can finish in two periods. The child arguing for three periods pointed out that half a period would go in explaining the drama to Bhumika who was absent the previous day. The children decided to explain the play to Bhumika before the class began. Bhumika herself suggested a compact plan with time calculation, something like a lesson plan a teacher is supposed to prepare beforehand.

The children also argue and negotiate with other groups if they are assigned a facilitator and try to convince them to reschedule the class.

After planning, the children move to the thematic rooms in groups.

The thematic areas

Knowledge exists within a context. We do not perceive it as different subjects in real life. We have rooms for a specific area of enquiry. For example, the school has a room for language. This doesn't mean language can be learnt only in this room. Language exposure happens everywhere in the school. But the room was set up to collect and organize resources to facilitate activities to learn language. Similarly, the school has other thematic rooms for enquiry into other areas of knowledge where resources and materials for that area of enquiry are collated. The rooms are not named after the subject areas they broadly focus on because children tend to wander beyond the conventional understanding of subjects. They include the following:

1. Room for Language & Enquiry

2. Room for Numeracy and Logic

3. Room For Art and Aesthetics
   a. Visual Arts
   b. Performing Arts

4. Room for the Child Scientist

5. Sense of History and Society

6. Space for physical activities & Health

Apart from being equipped with resources, each room is assigned a skilled facilitator with expertise in that particular field of enquiry, who is ever sensitive to the interests, level and pace of individual students and is ready to change/ mould activities accordingly. All the rooms look attractive thanks to the facilitator's personalized arrangements and decoration. The room names are written in coloured lettering on card sheet strips that are stuck on the door. The facilitators organize their personal sitting space and well as other furniture, racks, cupboards, boards, charts activity materials and so on. Below is a brief sketch of the rooms.

Room for Language & Enquiry

When you enter the room you find the walls filled with posters of stories, rhymes and songs that the children prepare while working in the room. There are soft boards that have children's questions and written work on them. A carpet is spread in the room with a couple of tables with chairs in one corner. The chairs are strong and handy and children can easily carry them to different rooms. There is also a library with around 2,000 books (Hindi and English), mostly story books. The room has all the materials needed to prepare and execute language activities and display the children's work. It also has sufficient material for the facilitator's personal study and interest.

Stories, drama and songs are central to the developmental strategy for this area of learning - talking, listening, making stories, enacting them and writing them.

We do not go into the complexity of learning isolated alphabets. Neither have we designed, structured and sequenced skill acquisition (listen, speak, read and write), but we start with all four skills together. I was firm on the idea that text is only a small part of language and text-based learning can be a difficult journey for a child. We need to focus, instead, on language learning in a more holistic way and creatively design activities for the purpose. So we expose children to the world of language through oral communication along with bringing in the textual form of what they hear and speak. Every child has her/his own path of acquiring skills so we widened the reference points, focusing on developing other language properties as well. I shall discuss this in detail later in the chapter on language acquisition.

I believe the most productive discussions emerge from social enquiry. That's how we decided the name 'Room for Language and Enquiry'. Fortunately, we found a facilitator Stephney D'vas who shared a similar approach. I communicated my ideas to her and left everything in her hands to evolve the room. Our regular sharing and feedback helped improve the room and its methodology. Additional platforms like the podium and informal communication helped foster the children's language skills. They are fluent with oral language and the older children have learned to read and write.

Multilingual environment – Most ANDS children speak dialects of Hindi at home and some speak other languages as well. So, by default, the group is multilingual.

We attempted to use this multilingualism as a strength. We opened platforms where children can communicate in their language of comfort and understand issues and concepts from the perspective of other languages. During the morning gathering, children sing songs in different languages and dialects.

Exposure to English has come as demand from parents and serves the children well in the real world. We have a declared language policy:

> There will be space for the children's home language in the classroom process. They will also be able to learn Hindi and English with proficiency. They will be given resources in these languages as the main content languages.

To learn English, I believe the children should learn to converse in English. We organize special interventions to give them such exposure and the children are now picking up the language.

Room for Numeracy and Logic

This room's ambience is different. It is filled with a profusion of teaching-learning materials. Blocks and rods of different sizes, dice and counters, board games, logic games, puzzles etc lie in open cupboards. One wall has a string of colour-coded beads, with the beads arranged in groups of ten, and tags of numbers from 0 to 100 hanging in rows. I usually ask visitors to place a number tag on a particular number position on the string. I then place a number tag nearby. I ask them what they did before placing their number tag. The usual explanation is that they counted from 1, or jumped by tens and so on to reach the number. On my part, I tell them I placed my tag using their number tag as a starting point. This small negotiation suggests there could be 2-3 ways of interpreting and working with numbers.

We adults cross check our positioning of tags by different methods, but children don't have that many methods developed yet so they take some time in confirming using the minimal number sense they have, whether they have placed their tag properly. Their confidence with numbers is yet to develop. We need to spend a lot of time exposing them to numbers in different ways and let them develop different 'number' meanings. Whereas, in a conventional class, we share the symbol and name of the number and expect the child to develop the meaning of 'number'.

We have collected several board games that help children to acquire these different meanings of number. Changa-Astha is one such game similar to Ludo. Assume we use two dice and let four children play the game. If a child throws 4 and 3 with the dice she adds 7 and moves her counter 7 squares. If she moves to the 8th square by mistake her co-player immediately corrects her. In this way, 4 children do around 20-to-40 addition sums in an hour, that too mentally, correcting each other, and learn number sense in the process. Secondly, children decide which counter to move with each toss of the dice according to their winning strategy, which means they get a chance to exercise logical thinking.

That's why we call the space a 'Room for Numeracy and Logic'. We could not initially find a good teacher so the room's growth was weak compared to the language room but it got a boost when Ankit Singh joined us. Ankit has become a good friend of the children and picks up new ideas in mathematics teaching-learning very fast. As a result, no child at ANDS is afraid of mathematics, unlike in most conventional schools. They enjoying the subject and learn fast. I shall discuss this learning in detail later in a separate chapter.

Room for Art and Aesthetics

Resources, exposure and opportunity are three basic ideas at the core of this room. It is an art lab where the facilitator is a person with artistic ability who enjoys spending time in the room, creating works of art and sharing the joy of creation with the children. Our objective is to communicate this sense of joy. If children enjoy the act of creation our task is more than half done. They are instinctually creative - all we need to do is fill the room with resources and tools and leave the child free to draw, paint, sculpt or make a model. We also help develop their aesthetic sense by exposing them to artistic techniques and forms, including great works of art.

The **Visual Arts** room is full of cutting and pasting tools and art and craft materials such as colouring and painting materials, chart paper, colour paper, drawing sheets, soft rubber, rubber bands, scissors, cutters, etc. The creations of the children, which visitors find fascinating, are displayed in the room.

Children love colours and every child is a painter by birth. Four-year-old Ananya drew some circular shapes and said she has drawn a fairy flying in the sky. She imagined the fairy and attempted to draw it on paper. Her drawing is crude because her motor skills are yet to develop and she has no exposure to colour combinations. At this stage, it is important to validate her imagination and let her improve her motor skills. If she sustains her interest, she is sure to achieve greater command over her motor skills and colour combinations, which would definitely lead to an improved visual representation of her imagination.

People have observed that ANDS children give importance to art in their learning. Parents tell us they have seen their own kids collecting sundry items they can use for their art and craft creations. I have already given you the example in the introductory pages of this book of my daughter fashioning a doll with the help of an empty cold drink bottle. There are many such examples one comes across at ANDS and most of the children have a collection of their creations at home.

Pool of artists – Namita Jha was the one who set up the visual arts room. She has a background in painting and encouraged children to make free drawings, sharing her knowledge of art techniques, brush strokes and colour experiments with them. Satish Bhasker, the facilitator of the 'Room for the Child Scientist' also helped to expose children to art and craft by focusing on building working models using waste material, an activity they enjoyed. Both facilitators were good in their respective fields and enjoyed working with children, even helping them build their models.

This experience made us realise that limiting the 'Room for Art and Aesthetics' to a single facilitator would limit the art forms and styles. That made us think of building up a pool of artists. This means the school has not just one art teacher but a group of artists. We worked out a mutual agreement with local amateur and professional artists to come periodically to facilitate art activities for the children to expose them to a range of art styles. This pool includes a few parents and college students as well.

The **Performing Arts room** has a variety of musical instruments. It materialized when Varsha, who has a background in music and history, joined the school. All our children enjoy singing and listening to music and our school day starts with assembly singing. We often hear them singing through the day and a few have turned out to be melodious singers. They can even sing classical ragas (Desh raag). If ANDS children attend a home function or party you can be sure they will give a performance, singing without much hassle. If their number is large enough, they will even dominate the party with their singing.

Drama – Children in different groups often enact stories in Hindi and English. Many of these plays are presented to the whole school or performed in school functions. Sometimes the children decide to improve them further and have even held a couple of public shows outside the school.

We improvise a lot when turning stories into plays. Let me share the story of '*Geet kaa kamaal*'. The children selected this story after doing a couple of team building activities. They began rehearsing the play once they understood the situation and the story well. Gradually, songs were added and dialogues and acting polished on the basis of feedback from facilitators and other colleagues. The improvisations continued even into the final stage performance. This was illustrated by an interesting incident. We had an improvised stage with the boundaries marked by chalk. A very young child walked on stage and then walked off. Nobody bothered. At that moment the actress was telling her husband, *Ballu ke abba, aap jaakar so jao* (Ballu's father, you go to bed). Just then the child walked on stage again. This time the actress immediately improvised a dialogue *Ballu, tum yahan kya kar rahe ho, jao tum bhi jakar so jao.* (Ballu, what are you doing here, you too go to bed).

Room for the Child Scientist

This room is similar to the Art and Aesthetics room to some extent. It also has cutting-pasting tools as well as a jumble of other tools and materials - hammer, saw, pliers, nails, drinking straws, empty refills, syringes, injection bottles, ice-cream sticks, etc. The children are too young to learn and perform rigorous science experiments at this age but they enjoy making working toys and science models. As mentioned earlier, Satish initially focused on helping them make toys like paper fans, knifes and whistles using ice-cream sticks and so on. They were also inspired by easily available books and internet resources, with Satish encouraging and guiding them. Children enjoy tinkering and sometimes even design their own simple but original toys.

Another part of the room has elementary science kits and equipment such as a weighing scale, microscope, lenses, mirror strips, beakers, test-tubes, etc. These are used in experiments that expose the children to their environment and the natural world - flowers, plants, the animal kingdom, and so on. We initiated many such activities - making a rain gauge, making their own leaf collections, etc - some of which couldn't be sustained for long.

One activity that we managed to sustain is the 'tree friend' we mentioned earlier. The children first see a film 'The giving tree', in which a human demands one thing after another and the tree keeps giving till it dies. The children get emotional, one even cried. This triggers them to cultivate friendship with one tree in the campus. They hug it, clean the space around it and carefully observe it, seeing who else it shelters. They make bark prints and write poems, even celebrating their tree's birthday. We make a folder to collate their work.

My interest is to let them observe the outer structure and design of a plant, which they relate with other plants around. Working in groups also encourages them share information. For example, those more familiar with local plants and trees tell the others their names, uses and stories about them. Some others who are good at organizing the material contribute with those skills.

In addition, we organize air and water-related experiments and explorations around plants in the school garden. Children also do elementary air, light, sound and pressure experiments but without going into much conceptual explanations because they are too young. But we do encourage them to give their version of what happens in these experiments, ask questions and think more logically. We do not reject any question they ask and try to answer them. Sometimes we suggest simple ways for them to investigate and find an answer at their level.

In the third year, as the children grew older, they started taking an interest in doing long term activities as well. We had a discussion and prepared a question box which children drop their questions. We once shared the questions in the school announcement time, couple of children in groups have taken the responsibility to work further on the questions. One question was "how the butterfly gets the beautiful wings?" the team selected the question is now developing a 3D model to explain the life cycle of butterfly.

Sense of History and Society

This room emerged when Varsha joined the school. Initially it was part of the 'room for language and enquiry'. This initiative registers questions children naturally ask about society. The facilitator discusses their questions with them and encourages and guides them to explore the answers. For example, the children once started with the questions "How was the earth formed?" "Where did we come from?" The facilitator held a number of interactive classes, showing films and discussing the big bang, early human activities and so on. The children even visited the prehistoric human shelters and rock paintings at Bhimbetka near Bhopal.

Once they were discussing India's freedom movement. One child asked: "Didn't the Englishmen realize the pain that freedom fighters must have gone through when they were hanged?" The facilitator gave them a task of writing their feelings if they were the banyan tree where freedom fighters were hanged.

Space for physical activities and health

The entire school is effectively a space for children to play games and sports that help them to stay healthy. This is also because after every mental activity the children require spend time in sport and game to let them imbibe whatever they gone through as mental exercise. They get structured and unstructured opportunities to play and enjoy with friends and the faculty. The school infrastructure is designed to let children explore. As we mentioned earlier, the campus includes a splash water pool, sand pit, various outdoor games and playground equipment made of used tyres – swings, standing see-saw and trolley on tracks. We recently converted a garage into a sports room.

The facilitator

The room allotted to facilitators for their area of enquiry is their personal space in which they collect and organize resources and plan the sequence of activities for children to come and work with them. They take pride in their rooms and feel a sense of ownership, which is a motivating factor.

Quite naturally, they get to know every inch of their rooms intimately and can even locate a pin if they need it. It's like if I have a kitchen where I do my cooking. If my friends come to visit me and I prepare tea for them, I know exactly where the sugar and tea leaves are and reach for them more or less automatically. It's the same for the facilitators in their room. They keep collecting materials to add to their resources. So they are seldom short of resources for the planned activities and the range of materials is such they can plan a wide range of activities.

Take the example of one of my math classes. I had planned to let children play an exchange and addition game using matchstick bundles. But half the children did not like the activity and said they didn't want to continue playing the game. So we discussed the matter and decided by consensus to play Changa Astha, an indigenous game similar to Ludo played with a board, two dice and counters. It gives opportunities to add numbers. We had material readily available in the room and quickly organized the change-over for the children. So we had two different activities going on in the room simultaneously but pursuing the same math concept.

ANDS is a learning organization for the facilitators as well. Since the children choose activities from the list the facilitators prepare, there are often more than one choice. So at any given point of time it is quite likely that 3-to-5 activities are being pursued in the room. The facilitators get enough spare time to catch up on their reading and prepare their suggestions for the next round of activities. They work independently but support and cooperate with each other, sharing suggestions and ideas and learning together. There are also platforms to give them feedback on their work and other inputs.

The school team – My first task after I left Eklavya and found a building to house the school was to look for a person to help take care of the building and set up the school team. Vijay Jhopate had worked in the Eklavya library as a volunteer. I knew he was a hard working person so I asked him if he would be interested in joining me and appointed him as a caretaker in December 2011. He has since taken up a big chunk of the school administration, overseeing the renovations we undertook and even starting an evening library for children living in the colony where the school is located.

I then began my hunt for the school academic team. I had told my friends about the school so the word got around that we were looking for people to join us. We organized a mela on February 14, 2012 to give people an idea of what we planned to do and to spot potential talent for the school faculty. One of those who came to enquire was a friend of mine, Stephney D'vas, who had completed a Bachelor in elementary education from Delhi. Another was Satish Bhasker, a chemist in a water plant who did not like working as a chemist and was open to working in an unconventional school. He was good at making working science models. Stephney and Satish were appointed as facilitators for language and science respectively. Namita Jha, an amateur artist who is part of our core team, agreed to be the art facilitator. We now had the nucleus of an academic team so we began the first academic session of our school on April 1, 2012 with four children.

Stephney took the lead in organizing the day-to-day academic activities with me. She got the ball rolling. Satish brought many small working toys and helped the children make them while Namita let the children explore with colours. Visitors were immediately attracted by these two activities. Vasanti Deshmukh joined us as the math facilitator, an area in which our inputs were weak at the time. We had admitted some very young children who needed special attention and care. This is when Namita Bhagat joined as an apprentice/paid intern and soon became an active member of the ANDS team.

Varsha joined us in September 2013. She has a background in history and music so she began exploring songs and ragas for children so her entry led to the creation of our Performing Arts room and she soon became a part of the school's decision-making team. Unfortunately Stephney, Satish and Vasanti left for personal reasons so we had no language, science and maths facilitator. We advertised these vacancies and around two months later Nidhi Solanki joined us as a language facilitator. She was an asset but unfortunately she, too, left within six months.

A new dimension to language and the performing arts was added when Anil Singh joined us in January 2014. He has been working in education for a long time and is a parent as well. He left his earlier work, and now was working as a freelancer when we asked him to join us. He is a story teller and his stories were a fresh input into language learning and drama. He also became part of our decision-making team. We now needed a Math and English facilitator. We again advertised and Ankit Singh and Shikha Bansker joined us. Ankit's openness and my ideas gave a boost to mathematics pedagogy. Namita decided to limit her role from being a full time facilitator to working part time. That's when we began pursuing the idea of building up a pool of artists for art input.

Let me now share some thoughts about the facilitator journey and its direction in the school. We organize opportunities for potential candidates to work with children, after which we discuss the ANDS methodology with them. This interaction gives us some idea of their attitude to the 2-3 parameters I have in mind when selecting facilitators. They should like children and make friends with them easily. They should be open to new ideas. They should also be proficient in their area of enquiry.

Selected candidates are appointed on a temporary basis. This gives them time to familiarize themselves with the school, get comfortable with the school team and find their niche. We begin with the idea of thematic rooms and children planning their day's schedule and moving from one room to the next. They learn more about the role a good facilitator plays in a democratic environment of discussions, exchange of ideas and feedback and mutual support and cooperation.

Take the example of Namita Bhagat. The day she joined the school, she was asked to help the facilitator and cook food for the school. The second day she asked me: "What should I do, I have completed the worked assigned to me." I said: "I don't know." She was shocked. She never came back to me with this question. She started interacting with children on her own after finishing her work. They would demand she narrate a story. She made some effort to do this. I observed her interactions and gave some feedback. Her work profile has now changed. She is a junior group facilitator. Her story-telling has improved significantly. She was also encouraged to read books such as 'Totochan'.

Similarly, Vijay moved from his job as a caretaker and account keeper to a larger role. He is also part of school decision-making team. Nidhi has developed new ambitions in life. A student of physics, she joined the school to utilize her leisure time till she got engaged. Now she's interested in learning more and studying further in education.

I am not an administrator but a 'children facilitator' by nature so I had no idea how to move ahead. I would consult with the team for each and everything and proceed on the basis of the consensus reached. I never instruct anyone but let people come up with what they feel is good in any particular situation. Of course, when it comes to how children learn, I have a firm view: we will not force any child. We had hot discussions about the teaching-learning process. I hold the view that language is much more than the text, which is just a small part of learning. We continue our discussions and negotiations. Fortunately, we manage to work according to children's interest and their learning pace.

School feedback meetings: This platform plays a significant role in the growth of the school, its academic programme and the personal development of the facilitators. Children leave by 3.00 pm. The facilitators then sit together to share and discuss what happened during the school day. We usually start by singing songs that create a sense of 'we together shall create a difference' as self-motivation to keep exploring creativity in teaching. We then narrate our stories of our interaction with the children. This hour provides a number of inputs and directions for self-improvement and for improving the school.

One concern in the present educational system is that teachers are de-motivated. One reason is their isolation as professionals. The evening feedback meeting serves to break this isolation. The facilitators share their excitement about what happens in their interactions with children and exchange innovative ideas of how to work with them.

For example, one day I shared the mechanism of solving the 'who will go first' issue. Interestingly, I'd never heard the opposite 'who will not go first' view. Anyway, I asked the children to point a finger at the person they wanted to send first, excluding themselves. The person most children point to was chosen. Other facilitators have evolved their own methods. One randomly picked a name from a collection of name-slips, like a lottery. Another used a childhood rhyme *'Akkad bakkad bambe bou, assi nabbe poore sou'* to select the person to go first. He said the children improvised by adding their own words to the rhyme. Yet another said they proceed alphabetically. Another version was to have a race, with the children running to touch the facilitator and running back, the winner being the first.

The distilled learning is to use any of three methods - random selection, selection by voting, and selection based on a specific property or skill.

One day a facilitator shared her frustration that the children did not listen to her. We discussed her case and gave her feedback and suggestions. One pointed out the problem may be transitory and they would eventually listen to her. It was math class and one suggestion was to use 'tambola', a group game, to get the children to learn about number properties. This helped her develop a rapport with the children. I helped her add more such board games and activities, such as a 'shopping mall' activity, to get children interested in working with numbers.

The facilitators share ideas on how content should flow in different themes, how the syllabus should advance, what parents say, and resource demand/supply for upcoming activities. They are also self-critical, pointing out that they shout at children or get frustrated when an activity does not proceed in the projected way. Often, the reasons turn out to be personal. They feel encouraged when others point out that 'x' activity is interesting or they are reminded that 'y' activity seems incomplete and so on. Other issues discussed include upcoming functions and events, the direction in which the school is going and allocating responsibility for bringing out our Akriti newsletter. Everything is noted in a feedback diary.

I see the meetings as a space for assessing and tracking the growth pattern of individual child, an aspect I'll discuss in detail in a later chapter.

The school environment

One of ANDS' biggest assets is the open environment that we nurture, based on trust and understanding of the learning process in children, which impacts the functioning and activities for the school.

The premises: The different theme rooms give the school the look of a colourful playroom. The innovative activities of creating from waste material (*kabaad se jugaad*) attract the children. The theme-based design makes switching from one learning area to another easy and smooth. The space is flexible and we change the room settings frequently to bring in newness, the children participating in the process, which gives them a sense of ownership.

Every room has unique materials and the space is organized according to the nature of work. For example, the art and aesthetics (visual arts) room displays paintings and has lots of cutting/pasting tools and craft materials. The room for the child scientist has working models of science toys and materials for conducting experiments in the lab and the school garden. The walls of the school are filled with charts prepared on the line-diagrams made by young children as back ground. There are also display spaces where the children and facilitators put up their 2D and 3D creations.

The school design and schedule do not permit the children to spend their whole day in a single room – they move from one thematic room to another. Children are mobile and free to move around the school premise, which reflects their freedom of choice to study or not on a particular day. Yet their interest and motivation to learn is sustained. This voluntary involvement is linked to the pedagogy, with children learning in groups in a play-like atmosphere free of rigid rules and restrictions, their learning and language closely linked to their everyday life.

Take this small example. One day, the children were making a collage using paper strips, each with their own design. One child took more time than scheduled to complete her collage because it had a lot of elements in it. The theme based system saw the other children leaving at the end of the scheduled time for the next room. But she continued until she finished her collage before going to join her group little late.

Low weight bag – Students should be spared the heavy burden of carrying books in their satchels. That's a decision we took. We provide all the reading material at school and the children need to bring only their lunch box, water-bottle, worksheets and personal stuff.

Personal cupboard: A home has wardrobes and cupboards for books and other things. In school, every child has a personal shelf in the cupboards where they can keep their belongings. You may find a broken toy, stone collection, dry flower, bottle, empty matchbox, piece of wood piece, paper cutting, photographs of their favorite cartoon characters and what not. The children also keep their craft creations and paintings, worksheets, notebooks and other materials they work on in their room activities. It's also where they keep their satchels.

Children-adult relationship: This is a crucial aspect. Children and adults make mistakes and learn from their mistakes. Although smaller in body size with developing mental faculties for logic and reasoning and limited social exposure to use as reference points to understand issues, children are still capable of understanding some basic principles of living in society. They are curious about the world and everything in it. If they are in a free environment, the will use their time productively to explore what is new around them. You need to trust them.

Take the example of a three-year-old who saw a pair of scissors in the room for the child scientist and tried using it, although she was not with any group. I was in the room doing my work so I asked her if she would like to join her group. She said no. It was probably the first time she was cutting random strips of paper with the scissors and she was fascinated. It was like a magic for her so she just went on cutting. An adult would probably think she was wasting her time and making the room untidy, or may hurt herself. I asked her whether she would collect and throw the strips in the dustbin if not going to use those for. She nodded. I went back to my work. I hear some sound of pulling a box,

I turned to her she was pulling a dustbin and was actually collecting every single strip to drop in the bin.

I observed she was careful not to hurt herself. Children age 3-4 freely use sharp tools like scissors and paper cutters but not a single child has been hurt in three years of such activity in the school. We tell them to be careful and they do take care. We also tell them there is proper medical care available if they get hurt. I don't claim our instructions or reassurances reduce the possibility of an incident but they do have life experiences of being cut by something sharp so they take care. In such a situation the adult has to decide. Should the child be free to use the scissors or should she be stopped for fear of hurting herself? It requires trust to let the child free. This gives a such wonderful exposure to her.

We do not also intervene in everyday disputes among children and adults unless they ask. We do not pass a judgment but resort to '*baatcheet*' (discussion). We listen to both sides and point out possible consequences, then leave it to them to decide and move on.

Policy and rules: We have no rigid policy of how children and adults should function. Every policy and rule is open to question. We have a concept of flexible timing. The children can come late but the school activity will start on time. Adults are expected to inform us if they cannot come on time, especially those responsible for the morning activities. They are expected to assign their task to a colleague.

Flexible timings for adults is a subject of hot discussion as I write this book. One group insists on fixing the arrival time in the morning. I am the only one who opposes it, pointing out we can find specific solutions for specific problems, like we can rotate people or change responsibility to give someone a break. Although we have made some such attempts we have yet to work out an acceptable solution. Let's see how we move on this.

We have some firm rule as well. The school gates are not locked but no child can go outside the school boundary. We firmly communicate this, giving examples of adverse incidents. We do go out in groups if the children plan it. Fighting, bullying and teasing are frowned upon as objectionable, especially if the targeted child objects. That is when we intervene. A few incidents do come to our notice, some of which we ignore. The children have their own mechanism to solve such problems and there are always a couple of children who keep an eye out for such cases and jump in before it reaches us.

The inclusive school: The term inclusive stands for schools where children of all economic classes, castes and attainment levels study together. The RTE Act 2009 advocates inclusive education but the reality is something else. Some schools admit children from a lower economic background because of the 25% reservation clause in the act. However, there is no system to include them in existing classes or to retain them in school. The democratic school is truly inclusive.

I use the term specifically with reference to economic inclusion. Today, schools are available at graded price points. This means the quality of your child's education depends on the money you earn. If parents can only afford low education fees they can get their child admitted to only private/government schools with minimum facilities. There are schools with huge campuses and buildings, AC rooms, clean and neatly designed premises, transport facilities, electronic equipment and a variety of other resources. They are for the children of parents who can pay the higher fees they demand. These two examples are of schools at the two extremes of the range available.

All these schools have more or less the same perception of education and the methods for handling children. But the children they admit have different life experiences depending on their economic status.

ANDS is structured to implement the concept of inclusion in actual practice. Students enjoy equal opportunities and can participate and claim ownership of the school irrespective of their economic background, caste, creed, gender or attainment levels. Every student, including the differently abled, gets opportunities to explore the world around, live in a community, participate in decision-making and become active self-learners. This inclusiveness is seen as a cultural resource in the school. We have children from all economic backgrounds, not just the elite or the lower economic group. Our fee structure is a model of inclusive education, with full and partial fee waivers based on the income and size of the family. In 2014, we had 28 children, 11 paying full fees - 6 free students, 5 paying token fees and 6 paying 25-to-50% of the statutory fees.

ANDS has been able to keep children from different socio economic backgrounds together even if their values sometimes clash. For example, they are either over conscious or reluctant about cleanliness. During these years we have seen a positive movement from both extremes. To illustrate this, I would like to share an example. Some children from silently better-off families never played with optimum strength, they seemed to scare of getting injured. But when they saw children of same age group played without fear and enjoy the game their ball-through was in line and powerful. We saw dramatic change within few months, the children also learn the technique of perfect through by themselves and also over roughness of some children also reached to balanced state.

The ANDS experience suggests that the democratic school model is the best answer to battling social differences in education. In the democratic model, children have a stake in school processes so the pedagogy structures learning according to their interest, pace and life experiences. Activities cannot be de-contextualised so they learn to share and discuss experiences in their home language.

Learning methodology - We believe children are capable and autonomous by nature. They observe, interact with everything, think and learn on their own from their surroundings at their pace and according to their interest. But the conventional school focuses on 'factual information' and follows a 'linear and uniform method of teaching', 'treating children as inanimate raw material to be processed into finished goods'. As a result, they are not able to achieve basic skills or exploit their potential in school.

Take the example of language teaching, which is an essential part of all schools at all levels. Surveys show that most children in primary schools are not able to read basic texts and when they do succeed in this skill, most of them lose interest in reading. At ANDS, most 7-year-olds now read and write with comprehension. We do not pressurize children to learn things in a uniform sequence. The free environment encourages language learning and the development of numerical abilities so we are able to finish and even go beyond the official curriculum set by education authorities.

Children's 'mistakes' are projected as shameful in conventional schools and they are humiliated and punished. ANDS does not condemn the mistakes but see them as genuine efforts to understand. For example, children were pasting name slips on various plants. One child wrote '*Toolsi*' (for Tulsi) in Hindi. The facilitator ignored the mistake and it was flagged on the '*Tulsi*' plant for many days. When her friends read the name, they pronounced it as written so the child realized her mistake and probably corrected it in her mind. I believe that there are n different means for a child to get to realize her mistakes. We have many such examples of 'mistakes' not stopping children from forging ahead. During the last three years, we have experimented with communication and pedagogical processes that allow children to learn at their own pace and interest to their optimal potential in all areas of enquiry.

ANDS provides children with an encouraging environment for self expression, including a special platform for addressing school gatherings. We called it the Podium and have made it a part of the daily morning assembly of all pupils and school staff. It's a forum where children are encouraged to share their experiences of the previous day with others. It's not only an effective way of giving children the opportunity to overcome their inhibitions in public speaking, but also a means for us to assess their involvement in school processes.

The children: A school run by children is one of our ambitious agendas. We have yet to form a clear picture of how exactly it will take shape. Our children have a stake in the school's activities. Nothing is forced or imposed on them. Even in academics we share with them what activity we plan for them and discuss the matter. They then have the option to discard or amend our suggestions.

We have attempted to let children participate in other decision-making processes in the school as well. We started school meetings where the entire school sits together and discusses the school's functioning. The assumption is that children and adults should have equal rights in discussing school issues. In the first meeting, the children pointed out that chocolate wrappers litter the school so two of them, along with a facilitator, decided to make a special chocolate wrapper bin. Another group decided to make plastic and non-plastic bins for other garbage. We had couple of other meetings. But, by and large, I would say they were unsuccessful in creating a momentum for taking up more responsibilities or at least participating in school activities and decisions.

When the parliamentary elections were under way in Bhopal, a group of children asked about the election and discussed the issue in the 'sense of history and society room'. They were interested in knowing whether they could also participate in the election. In the subsequent feedback meeting, the facilitator suggested we conduct an election to let them understand the election process. We thought this may give a boost to our ambitious agenda of children's participation in the school's functioning. We decided to make our 'election' as realistic as possible. Anil was given the responsibility to lead.

It was a month-long process. Anil put the proposal of holding an election before the children in a discussion with them. The children agreed on a polling date and decided to form committees, which included the Vyavastha Samiti (logistics committee), PadhaI Likhai Samiti (committee for learning), Chhapai Samiti (printing committee), Medical Samiti (medical committee), Ladai-Jhagada Niptana Samiti (dispute settlement committee), Khel Samiti (sports committee) and Aayojan Samiti (organizing committee). There were nomination forms and a withdrawal date, with one child withdrawing. They organized the campaign, delivered speeches and put up posters in the school. We had a mock election before the election date. Then we had the final election. It was interesting to see the results. The children aspiring for the post of their choice got the highest votes for that post, with their rivals far behind, but received few votes for other posts.

Anyway, we now have committees with elected members and are in the process of giving the children some idea of the work they can do. It seems that this would move ahead and children may start participating in school management as well.

Children drop out

The parents reluctance to let their children continue studying in a non-conventional school despite their progressive view on education, strengthened by their demand for textual learning and measurable outcomes, led to a heavy drop-out rate at ANDS initially. The drop-outs were from all economic backgrounds. I found that although parents trust our academic methods, societal pressures forced them to change their mind. They failed to see what we classify as the achievements of the children and their learning outcomes. The questions they raised were: Children are always seen playing so when exactly do they study in school? Why don't they get written homework? Are the children learning anything?

The number of students in the school has grown nevertheless. We started with four children; their number grew to 12 by the end of the first year, goes to 22 the next year and touched 32 in the third year. Now there are 28 children at the moment in Dec 2014 with a hope to have more children in future.

Parent community

Since the beginning we were clear that ANDS should be a joint effort and not seen as a service institute or teaching shop run by a couple of people, with parents buying the services for their children for a fee. For us, learning doesn't start when the children enter the school campus and stop when they go home. It is a continuous process, with inputs from home, the school and society working together. So there should be communication and sharing between all stakeholders, with the parents' role being the best resource for the school in relation to their child's growth.

We began by sharing our thoughts about the school and its design with a couple of parents to encourage them to admit their children, along with our children. That's how we started with 4-5 students. We formed the first parents' group. Every time a parent came to enquire about the school I would conduct a detailed tour, explaining our teaching-learning method and the way the school functioned. We would have a question-answer session. This would clarify to them that the method of education here would be different. Only parents oriented in this way joined us by admitting their children. So the initial group of parents was aware of the pros and cons of conventional schools and alternative schools.

We try to make parents comfortable with the school activities and school team. There are no rigid boundaries for them and everything works on mutual understanding and trust. They move around the school and even visit their children during their school activities, of course getting prior permission and not disturbing the school rhythm. The children are comfortable with this as long as they are not bothered. We have informal and personal interactions with the parents, communicating our experiences. They also talk to the facilitators and attend feedback meetings and singing sessions. Informal chats over a cup of tea are also a good source of feedback, suggestions and comments.

We have formal meetings and child-focused discussions with individual parents when the summative assessment reports are shared with them. We take their suggestions and inputs seriously, especially adverse comments they make about the school and its functioning, initiating improvements on their basis.

One evening the parents of a child suggested organizing a meeting of the ANDS community (parents and school staff). One of the parents had circulated the invitation. We met one Saturday in an open meeting with no fixed agenda. At this we managed to maintain that the meeting is not called by school as authority but the meeting is a joint programme by parents and school. Every one shared the concerns and strengths and discussed the progress of the school. 'How can we help our child at home?', 'The total

Number of children in the school?' 'When will their child learn to read?', similar about mathematics, these were couple of genuine concerns, the ANDS community decided to work ahead. We decided to talk about specific concerns about the language education. We held a 2-3 hour workshop for the parents in which we shared our pedagogical understanding about 'how a child learns language'. We also opened the school reference library for them so they could help their children at home.

We decided to continue such meetings and called experts in education to the next meeting to discuss various educational issues with the ANDS community. We also had a couple of meetings to share the developments taking place in the school.

Another issue that helped strengthen parents' participation in the ANDS community was a discussion regarding the problems of children attending school during winter. Parents were concerned about the starting time because of the morning cold. Another concern was the total time the children spent in school. I encouraged a discussion on alternative timings. The discussion continued by email but was inconclusive so in the absence of a 'community' meeting the school team acted as a default group and took an ad hoc decision after ascertaining everyone's views. But the new timings were difficult to adhere to in the winter conditions. Also, parents questioned how far they should intervene in such decisions, although we were still open to further discussion.

I have no idea to what extent the parents' community can participate in the decision-making process. What are the other possible modes of involvement? Anyway, we felt the whole exercise was a good initiative instead of limiting the interaction and discussion to the school team and we are hopeful things will evolve over time.

Assessment method: The RTE says children should not be required to pass a board examination before completing their elementary education. This effectively means there should be no term-end or year-end examinations because children should not be subjected to the periodic tension of scoring good marks in examinations.

We drew up a plan for continuous and comprehensive evaluation (CCE), as suggested in policy documents on education, including our daily observations of the children. We note down what children say at the Podium every morning and build up an annual record that amounts to self-assessment. We also use peer-group assessments to keep a record of the children's progress. All this information feeds into making a comprehensive assessment of each pupil at the end of the academic year. The ANDS system of assessment is process-based and avoids examinations, in line with the RTE's vision. I will discuss this in detail in a separate chapter.

ANDS support structure: We have built up a network of people interested in education who are associated with the school and frequently visit to participate in conceptual brainstorming and classroom activities. This resource group consists of BElEd graduates and educationists associated with Eklavya, Samavesh and other NGOs and educational institutions.

These professionals provide resource inputs to the students so they can explore different dimensions of their interest areas including story-telling, theatre, music, pottery, painting, sculpture, clay modelling, paper mache, indigenous art and other crafts.

Dress code: The students can wear clothes of their choice to school. There is no uniform but a school apron/T-shirt is provided to every student, which they wear most of the time.

Achievements: I have already discussed successes stories at different points in this narrative. These achievements, based on empirical observations, are listed below:

- Children are happy at school and do not want to go back at closing time.
- There is significant improvement in their confidence levels.
- Even poor and challenged learners show improvement.
- The children gain good command over oral articulation.
- There is strong bonding among them.
- Their creativity, curiosity and sensitivity are nurtured.
- We ensure holistic development, including academics, art and games.
- We foster democratic and inclusive values.

Some activities and innovations

Mentoring: We recently introduced the idea of mentoring as the number of children in the school increased. Earlier, no one person had the formal responsibility for a group of children as their number was low so we could devote individual attention to all them. A mentor is like a class teacher. We have formed a small team and distributed the responsibility for mentoring different groups of children. The mentor takes care of all the records such as children's academic work, observations, anecdotes etc and updates the records to keep a track of their development. (S)he also communicates with the parents about their child's progress. The children can choose to their personal mentor to talk with personal issue who may be different than their group mentor.

We have initiated this process and have started collecting the children's work in files. We also visit parents, which is opening up new dimensions, the older children also participated in these home discussions. This process is at the initial stage and will take more time to improve.

School diary: Every child now has a diary which ensures more frequent and regular communication with parents.

Worksheets and syllabus: Part of the children's activities sometimes extends into their homes, which we call homework but is not actually additional work to be done at home. The work is different in nature – like finding different ingredients in your kitchen which you can use as colour and so on. Such tasks are also not regular so parents don't see them or surveys children undertake as homework. Also, most parents are not familiar with the learning methodology so they are not equipped to help their children at home.

So we came up with idea of worksheets. We prepare worksheets for children in different groups, which are usually a continuation of their theme room activities. The children always have 4-5 worksheets in their folder and can work on them anytime they feel like doing some school work at home. This system is still at the beginning stage.

We have also started giving a suggested syllabus for a month to the parents, although we were not sure whether we should move in this direction.

Sharing with community

Akriti newsletter: We share information with parents about the activities that the children do. But there is a lot more than activities that the children do in the school. So I began circulating a detailed note to parents that included anecdotes and observations about the children in addition to the activities they do. When Varsha joined, she converted the note into a school newsletter. It was a quarterly that discussed happenings in the school, mentioned the names of visitors to the school, and published extracts from the diaries of the facilitators as well as children's photographs, their creative contributions and group reports. We also produce our Akriti school magazine at the end of the year.

Marketing: We had a bad experience with our first marketing initiative because none of us had any experience in this area. We prepared a leaflet and distributed 8,000 copies, which generated only two inquiries. The leaflet was filled with stock phrases such as theme-based rooms, individual attention and stress-free education that every school mentions in its publicity material. So there was no point of differentiation.

We decided the only way to share our viewpoint about education and highlight the school's positive aspects was to bring people to visit the school. So we conducted painting workshops in residential communities with the help of some of our parents and displayed over 300 paintings in the school done by children of these communities. Only a few people turned up.

We regularly organize summer camps in the month of may, which, I think, was the only partially successful marketing initiative, resulting in a couple of admissions. We have also prepared a three-page brochure about the school and its work. But marketing remains a big challenge and is one area we need to do a lot more.

Financial backing: Till now we have received financial support from the Anand Niketan Group of Schools, Gujarat. Around 10-to-15% of our expenditure is generated from school fees, sponsorships and other means. We would also need to set up a team for research and advocacy, which would require separate funding.

Issues and challenges ahead

Financial sustainability: Our effort to become an inclusive school means we have a number of non-fee paying students. It's a constant battle for us to move towards at least partial financial stability and sustainability of the school.

Acceptance by society: The conventional perception of education - more information-based with measurable outcomes (examinations) – has acted as a barrier that stops parents from treading the unconventional path and taking a chance on their children. Students at ANDS learn and advance at their pace and interest so their achievement is comprehensive and holistic. They do achieve established outcomes, not in a grade-based format, but at their individual pace. For example, all our 6+ years children learn to read with comprehension, not by mechanically decoding alphabets and words, which is an advantage in their learning journey because they love reading and discover on their own new alphabets and worlds.

Ever-evolving process: We have been running ANDS for three years and have evolved innovative, activity-based learning processes apart from building up collections of activities and resources for different learning areas. Although we have crystallised our theoretical ideas in actual practice, we see the school as a work in progress and we still have some way to go to be able to influence educational policy and practices in schools.

Disseminating the idea

Web presence: I have started a blog and a Facebook page in which we post the latest developments, events and news about the school. The web addresses are:

http://anbhopal.weebly.com/
http://www.facebook.com/AnandNiketanBhopal?ref=hl

Print and online media: A few articles about ANDS have been published in magazines across India from 2012 onwards. They include:

- 'Anokha School' - Shiksha Ki Buniyad, January 2013, Vidya Bhawan Society, Udaipur;
- Khoje aur Jane (oct'14) and Shiksha Ki Buniyad (Oct 14) - http://teachersofindia.org/hi/ebook
- 'Anand Ka Ek Saal' - Khoje aur Jane, January 21, 2014, Vidya Bhawan Society, Udaipur; http://www.teachersofindia.org/hi
- http://www.beyondteaching.com/cache/eduupdate/623.php
- http://rajasthanpatrika.patrika.com/.......
- http://www.nayaindia.com/news/latest-news/wire-news............-257362.html on 8 feb 2014
- http://janoduniya.tv/tag/anand-niketan-democratic-school
- https://www.youtube.com/watch?v=3sMyrdvfwUk

Articles which later turned in to chapters of this book - "teacher plus" Feb' 15 http://www.teacherplus.org/interventions/a-dream-realized, and Contemporary Education Dialog expecting in July'15

Shows on Radio & TV about School in 2013

- ANDS on Radio Vividh Bharti, Bhopal on 28 feb 2013;
- ANDS on Radio Mirchi, Bhopal on 15 July 2013 ;
- ANDS on TV; "Pahal" of Bhopal Doordarshan on 24 oct'13 https://www.youtube.com/watch?v=3sMyrdvfwUk

Many other articles about various aspects and are under publishing at different places.

Replicability of ANDS

The RTE advocates a common school system and requires private schools to reserve 25% of their admissions for underprivileged children. This implies that all schools have to be inclusive. A crucial issue is to create an environment in these schools to retain such students. The Natural Learning Model evolving at ANDS can be an answer to this since it caters to all sections of society.

In a Natural Learning model children have their stake in school processes hence it is inherent in the model to adopt a pedagogy where learning takes place according to the children's interest and pace. So existing schools can directly implement the ANDS ideas and methods and evolve their version of a Natural Learning model. I believe that This is an ever evolving Model can have various version depending on the people, time and environment.

Intervention at AIIMS campus: We are open to explore all possibilities and to support existing interventions. For example, two faculty members of the All India Institute of Medical Sciences have begun an initiative to start a learning centre 'Apna School' in the AIIMS campus for the children of contract labour. ANDS provides academic support for this venture.

I had also been visiting a private school for teacher and parent orientation. The school has recently started a period of Junkyard Science for older children with our support.

A proposal: I would also like to propose a project to support schools to develop language learning activities to develop the four language skills (listening, speaking, reading and writing) in the primary grades as a regular feature without disturbing their school schedule. These may be an hour-long activity for the children in different groups depending upon the school size and facilities.

The proposed intervention emerges from activities developed at ANDS and at the moment is at the level of proof of concept. The set of activities are:

- The Podium: A platform for oral expression
- The Children's Wallpaper: Strong source of motivation to read and write

Future aspiration:

- There is no finish line for ANDS, which I see as an ever-evolving model that documents its practices.

Hence, we would like ANDS to be a self-sustaining model of a democratic and inclusive school with a realistic methodology that is open-ended and activity-based and allows children to become active, self-directed learners.

- I would like ANDS to serve as an exploration and learning hub for individuals and professionals. We would like to encourage researchers to conduct studies, document their practices and share their innovations with educational communities.

- I would like to foster the setting up and development of more innovative schools so parents have the option to choose a school that suits their child's nature and style. Not all children can survive in an inflexible environment.

Experiences of language acquisition at ANDS

When will our child learn to read? This is one of the questions parents ask us. The answer, for us, goes beyond the conventional method of education and language learning.

Whatever we do at ANDS is what researchers in education say is the way children should learn. I have been part of the language learning discourse for many years and this exposure and my work with children have shaped my understanding of how children acquire language.

Conventional schools still use traditional methodologies for language learning. Children can communicate in their mother tongue when they are 3-4 years old yet empirical observations reveal that most students in primary schools cannot read basic text even after spending 4-5 years in school. I would like to share my insights and experiences into language acquisition and point to the need for reviewing current classroom practices in language education.

I find language acquisition one of the most fascinating aspects of a child's growing up and learning. By language I mean the home language (usually the mother tongue or first language) children use in their immediate environment. The process would differ in the case of acquiring a second language. In this chapter, I talk about my understanding of children's first language acquisition, which is Hindi in the situations I have worked in.

Problematizing the issue

There is a popular story about a parrot that was taught to be careful about traps. One day, it was caught in a hunter's trap and kept ranting, "We should be careful of traps, we should be careful of traps." The parrot could repeat what it was taught but didn't understand its meaning. All animals communicate in different ways. Only humans have the capacity to comprehend and communicate the abstract through language. Humans have evolved to develop language to connect and communicate in a complex social environment.

The NCF 2005 in its 'Executive summary of teaching of Indian languages' says: *'Language is not only a medium of communication but also a phenomenon that, to a great extent, structures our thought and defines our social relationships in terms of both power and equality."* Hence, language learning plays a vital role in the overall development of a child.

Language acquisition is a social process, not something that occurs in the individual mind alone. It is influenced by a child's surroundings, which create the need and provide the inputs for acquiring language. In other words, the cultural and social environment of the child plays a significant role in acquiring language.

Let me describe more about this. Children have an unfathomable capacity to learn a language. The ways in which they learn are more varied and complex than we imagine. Let's take the example of a four-year-old child who learns her mother tongue. If her mother tongue is English I don't think she would make any mistake in pronouncing the alphabets 'D' and 'T' and distinguishing between the two sounds. She is unlikely to say 'tate' instead of 'date', or 'dalk' instead of 'talk'. No child would be able to explain how exactly he/she has twisted his/her tongue to pronounce these alphabets with the precise difference. No one has taught tongue twisting to make appropriate sound to the child. This self-learning is true across languages. The child understands this complex system of sounds and how to produce them without being taught?

Children hear these sounds for most of their waking hours and use and play with them. In the early years after birth, it's only the affectionate responses of adults to their inchoate attempts that signal to them that they have successfully produced the correct sound. Children cannot read the language at this stage. They first try hard to decode language before reaching a stage where they can learn to read it.

How does this change occur?

Children live in a text-rich environment and start recognising words as pictures without decoding. When Amber was five years old, she could recognise the word 'Eklavya' but could not decode it by combining its different alphabets. She saw the word as a picture and must have built up many such word-pictures in her mind. To distinguish between word-pictures she would need to compare them and learn to recognize the different alphabets. That is how children learn the building blocks of language – the alphabets. In such an approach, they learn the alphabets randomly, not in the sequence prescribed in language textbooks. They learn to read even before they recognise all the alphabets. Amber learned to read when she was seven years old. The point to note is that every child has a unique learning trajectory.

So what does this insight into learning tell us? It's simple. We should expose young children to language, giving them every possible opportunity to express themselves, and respond sensitively to their every attempt.

Unfortunately, conventional schools follow a different path. Teachers compel children to memorise the alphabets given in a textbook. The text is de-contextualised, which means it has no connection with the children's life and environment. This approach is not in tune with the way children learn. Also, they learn in a trial-and-error process in which they frequently make mistakes. They get discouraged if their mistakes are pointed out in a way that humiliates them, without understanding and sympathy. That's what usually happens in a classroom. It de-motivates children.

We can sum up the shortcomings of this alphabet-based approach to learning language as follows:

Narrow perspective: Memorising alphabets and decoding text are only a small part of the vast arena of language learning but schools tend to focus exclusively on these aspects. One reason could be that acquisition of these skills is measurable so a child's progress can be quantitatively monitored. But other objectives such as language comprehension, expression, organization and articulation of thought and reflection are equally, if not more, important.

Elements in isolation: Children learn the alphabets in isolation as abstract symbols. There is no context or link to their real life experiences or their environment. Grammar is also taught in this mechanical way. I believe learning these in isolation may help us to focus on but one can learn these and other aspects of language comprehensively within the complete language setting. Frank Smith rightly says children do not learn to read through knowledge of the alphabet alone but they learn to read in a contextual, text-rich environment.

Linear design: Language learning is designed as a step-by-step progression based on some logical analysis of language. So you begin with the alphabets, move to two-letter words, then more complex words using vowels, on to simple two-word sentences and, finally, complex and compound sentences, with a study of the grammar of sentence construction woven into the process. This linear progression, imposed within the confines of the classroom, doesn't work too well with children.

The whole edifice of language learning in schools is built around these practices and approach and is now entrenched in the system, holding parents in its thrall, and fortified by examinations to measure the progress of children.

That's why I personally believe we need to take a holistic approach to language learning, de-emphasising de-contextualized learning and focusing, instead, on the child's instinctual learning patterns. It should be taken out of the confines of the classroom and situated in the child's world – the home, neighbourhood, school and so on. And we also need to create a text-rich environment to fortify and consolidate the learning process. Songs, stories and its enactment, social enquiry should become core learning content of the child.

That's what we have done at ANDS, moving away from the conventional methodology of language teaching-learning. Let me share some of our experiences of how children develop their command over language. These insights shaped my understanding of language acquisition by children. I will list them in sequence to build up the logic of how our children learn language and also give details of the environment the school has created to foster the their learning journey

Memorising alphabets?

There are no learning deadlines at ANDS. We don't insist that children learn a fixed quantum of knowledge in a fixed period of time. The activities for language learning are not sequenced and do not go into the complexity of alphabets. I personally don't agree that children should spend time memorising isolated alphabets but two children aged 5 years said they wanted to learn the alphabets first. They must have thought recognising the alphabet is crucial to read, which seems sensible. Since the children expressed the desire to work with the alphabet so we gave them the alphabet chart and the facilitator was there to help them, when needed. They wrote all the alphabets twice, then said they didn't enjoy doing this and dropped the idea for the time. Maybe they were looking for other ways to learn the alphabets but doing such exercises in isolation of a context is tedious and children soon get bored.

Instead, why can't teachers begin with more meaningful words and even sentences? For example, start with the child's name, their parents' name and so on. Most words have more than one alphabet so the children are exposed to alphabets and get to recognise them. It may not be in the textbook sequence but does that really matter? I remember one evening when my daughter was six years old. She was half asleep, suddenly woke up and asked how to write 'क' (a Hindi alphabet). I wrote it for her on a paper. She religiously copied it 5-6 times and went back to sleep. She must have had something on her mind which led her do this. What's important is that you should let children pursue their desires and interests.

Anyway, children soon learn to read, though it's difficult to tell how. The process could be different for each child, with some learning faster than others. Once a child learns, others realise it's do-able so they speed up their own efforts. It was this belief that all children create their own journey of learning that led us to expose them to stories and poems. We got encouraging results. Most of our 6+ years children learned to read within six months. The thing is not to interfere in this learning journey but to maintain a friendly and stress-free environment. The focus should be on creating more opportunities for language exposure instead of pursuing an alphabet-based learning methodology.

Curiosity catalyses the urge to learn

One day, a six-year-old child stayed back after the story-telling session. She was curious to know something from her teacher. "How is it when you tell a story from the book it's always the same, but when I tell the story from the same book it changes every time?" she asked. "I read the printed text in the book but you make up the story from the pictures," responded the teacher.

Just 15 days later, the child was 'reading' a story. I suppose her conversation with the teacher had developed in her a curiosity to know the mystery of the text. This created a strong urge to learn to read. Another child also developed the urge to read when she was not able to read the drama script along with her friends and we saw her making several attempts to learn to read. She would sit in a corner with the facilitators reading a book. She, too, learnt to read within a month. We saw that she read the script without help.

The children learn best on their own; at their own pace, reading a book that interests them. Even children in the same age group can be at different stages of learning the four language skills (listening, speaking, reading and writing). As a school, we can help them by creating the appropriate environment, organizing text-rich resources and ensuring their autonomy. We shouldn't interfere at the cognitive level. If children sense they 'don't know' they develop the urge to 'know' and look for the resources and opportunity to learn. They play with language to communicate with the world they live in, in the process acquiring the required skills.

Experiments with language

Children experiment with language in their attempt to learn. I'd like to share some observations of their 'play and experiment' with language.

I remember an experiment my daughter made when she was 4-5 years old. She had a ball and wanted to play catch with me. "*Papa, main phenkungi aap kechna,*" she said (Papa, I'll throw, you catch). Her use of the word '*kechna*' took me by surprise. It was her creation, a mixture of the English 'catch' (pronounced *kech*) and the Hindi '*na*', a suffix. We speak Hindi at home so English is not a language she's familiar with. She must have heard the word 'catch' in a conversation or a film and understood its meaning. She was familiar with verbs like '*doudna*' (running), '*koodna*' (jumping), '*khelna*' (playing), '*rona*' (crying) and '*nachna*' (dancing). She figured out how and where to use '*na*' and constructed the new word by adding the suffix to the verb '*kech*'. Top of all that, I salute to her conviction that she had figured out a suitable situation and used the word without hesitation and not for the sake of experiment but she actually wanted me to understand the game and want me to play with her.

Here's another example involving six-year-old Shatakshi. We use the words '*tumhara*' (yours) and '*hamara*' (ours) in Hindi. Shatakshi says '*tumka*' and '*hamka*' in her conversations. They are herown constructions. We have words in Hindi such as '*uska*' and '*iska*' (his) and '*kiska*' and '*jiska*' (whose). She picked up the '*ka*' and added it to '*tum*' (you) and '*hum*' (we) to get the possessive pronouns. She used the words confidently and was not 'corrected' in school or at home. We don't know how long she'll persist with the usage, but we aren't negative about her creations. In most schools, teachers would label it a 'mistake' and even punish her but in ANDS mistakes are seen as essential to the learning process.

Unfortunately "Mistakes" are sin in our schools and we have created this fear for mistakes by punishing or creating red marks or humiliating among others. I am proud to say that our children make mistakes at ANDS. The school should encourage the urge to learn and create opportunities to experiment and make mistakes by ensuring an environment and resources to foster learning.

How children advance

Mastering on or learning these skills are not children's objective at all but they wanted to get hold on the language to use and communicate it. In other words, these skills were just a by-product of the attempt for being able to communicate more meaningfully and precisely. Children play with language, experiment with sounds and words in ways that may not make sense to us. But they end up speaking, comprehending, reading and writing. The paths they take may differ, the pace at which they learn these language skills may differ.

Is there an underlying pattern to mastering these language skills? I have been observing children at ANDS and elsewhere to understand if there is a pattern. But my observations are limited to a period of 2-3 years with a small group of children in a specific environment so I cannot claim any pattern emerging out of them to be a 'universal pattern' of language learning. Nevertheless I would like to share some of these milestones;

Listening

When the auditory organs develop, a child begins recognizing sounds and turns her head in the direction of the sound. She begins storing the memory of different sounds and is able to recognize the differences. Second thing she may divide all of them into two categories people's voices and sounds from objects.

The child learns that responses to voices differ from responses to sounds from objects. The child would listen carefully and enact as if s/he understands the voice but I presume that they are curious to know how exactly these voices are produced and actually is capturing finer differences of voices. For eg. Saniya's, who stood blank when we told her something. The lack of the expected response made us realise she did not get what we wanted to communicate.

Some time children make a collection of responses from different children and adult and they just pick and copy one of them, which they found most suitable response for any communication it may look odd or irrelevant from an adult perspective. But they do improve as children grow older, listen more and their curiosity exposes them to more reference points in real life situations. I can only surmise that some logic based on observation and interaction as it operates beyond human limits at the cognitive level.

Oral language

Children communicate even at birth. They communicate by body language, facial expression, laughing or crying, shaking their head or hand, etc. I use the term 'bodily expression' for such communication. They gradually reduce bodily expression and increase verbal communication to fine-tune communication. But bodily expression – or body language – doesn't disappear and remains into adulthood. Now our body expressions add meaning to our communication

Speech is a remarkable development in children. Initially, they hear voices but cannot figure out how different sounds in those voices are produced by manipulating the tongue and vocal chords. These voices have some meaning for her and the child is interested in meaning. She wants to produce the meaningful voices in order to communicate. She, then, experiments in reproducing these sounds, first randomly, then with meaning to communicate. It is a trial and error process, every failure or mistake suggest to listen it carefully again, which is listening leading to more precision in reproduction and meaning.

The first meaningful words infants speak –'ममा'(mamaa) or 'ताता' (tata) – sends the parents into rapture. They don't bother about the precision of the voice. We joyfully share with friends that our child has spoken "ममा" (mamaa) or called me. This love gives unprecedented energy to the child and conveyed it to her that it was a meaningful voice and she would continue experimenting with sound producing different voices. Their loving response encourages the child to continue experimenting with sounds, which are now a strong tool to communicate with people around.

Children may lisp initially. The adult response should be clear and precise language exposure in response to the child else the lisp will persist little longer. Although later they certainly correct themselves from their surroundings. Children then learn more and more words by observation creative imitation and own creation. As they grow, the process speeds up and they learn oral language – words structured, sentences etc – through family, peer group and other social interaction.

The social environment plays a crucial role. Take my own example. I belong to central Madhya Pradesh where the sound 'स' (s) is used but 'श' (sh) and 'ष'(shh) are rare. Today, I still find it difficult to pronounce the sounds that were missing in my childhood, even after coming into contact with people living outside my region who are familiar with them. Similarly, the sound 'ळ'(something like alh) in Marathi and Tamil is difficult to learn in adulthood.

Communication is a combination of oral language and bodily expressions. One day, a child asked me छल पानी

Chhal pani (sir water) pointing to the *matka* containing water with her finger. She wanted me to give her a glass of water. The communication used two words of spoken language along with the body language of pointing as well as a distinct facial expression.

Gradually children start using more words and bodily expressions to communicate. I remember Khushi telling me 'हमाली छुट्टी 1 बजे' Hamali chhutti 1 baje (Our school is off at 1 o'clock). Although lisping ('l' instead of 'r'), she was trying to articulate a more complicated, almost complete sentence saying her school closes at 1 o'clock.

Children love adding to a sentence or completing an incomplete interrogatory sentence. I used to ask Khushi 'तुम्हारी छुट्टी होगी....' -Tumhari chhutti hogi....... (Your school will be off by.......). Khushi would immediately respond '1 बजे'- 1 baje (1 o'clock). Her answer shows she had comprehended and completed the unfinished query. Every time a child succeeds in communicating, she tends to repeat what she says, as if she is practising. She repeats joyfully, which shows she is keen to experiment further.

Children tend to talk a lot. They create new words, confidently using them in real life situations even if the words are not quite correct. They learn to emphasise some words and modulate their voice when speaking as part of their experiments in speaking and communicating meaningfully.

Discussions in school and outside play an important role in developing oral language. The children come across different words used in different contexts, derive meaning from these contextual sources, and practice these words with full conviction. I remember Prakriti, aged 4 years, learned the word 'idea' and would call me saying 'Should I give you an idea?' and she would place it in my palm. I don't know what she understood by the word but she later learnt to use it more precisely after hearing other adult usages of the word.

The influence of the context in the way children create words is illustrated in the following example. Shatakshi and Apramey were talking in the Visual Arts room. Shatakshi says: "I will become a craftor and make many crafts." Apramey responds: "You should become artor as you paint a lot." That's how real life situations help children build reference points, vocabulary, language patterns and grammar. I'm sure they learned the correct words later but that would be another story.

Children move on and learn to organize their thoughts before speaking, talking in a more focused and coherent manner and, at a later stage, analysing and using idioms and phrases. The process of using more precise and well-articulated doesn't stop - after all, the sky's the limit.

Reading

We have developed a highly text-rich environment at ANDS. Our language room has more than 2,000 books in Hindi and English. Children feel adults bring them superb stories from books. Or they see that reading is something interesting as older people spend considerable time in the library reading. They start picking up books, turning the pages and seeing the pictures. Gradually their interest shifts from pictures as they come to know the written text can also have meaning. They become curious to learn to read.

They start capturing the detail, for example that Hindi and English are read from left to right. Their fingers move left to right along the lines of the printed page. One day, a four-year-old girl was narrating a story from a book. She was making up the story from the illustrations. But her hand was moving along the printed text. Children pretend to read even if they cannot, which shows they have the urge to read.

This act of moving the finger along the text even without knowing how to read was seen in the case of another four-year-old girl. But here the underlying cause was different. Children often ask the facilitator to tell them the same story over and over again. They get to memorise every word of the story. So it wasn't surprising to see the girl 'reading' the story from the book but actually narrating it from memory while moving her finger along the text.

We have observed how children gradually begin to associate the illustrations with the text. They somehow point out the exact paragraph describing what the illustration shows and gradually get down to the exact lines and words. They associate the words-pictures they have memorised in their mind with the exact words in the line. For example, Prakriti often asked me to read picture stories (comics) in which she once came across the word 'भड़ाम' (bhadam) in a picture. She remembered the word as a picture, every time she came across the word in text she would stop me and read the word.

In the same way, children also remember words in the text as pictures and memorise them, building up a collection of word-pictures in their mind. As the collection grows, they learn to observe each word-picture in more detail and compare word-pictures so they can recall them when needed. For example, a child learns to recognize 'बेर' (ber, a fruit) and 'शेर' (sher, lion) as word-pictures but cannot decode them initially. But she compares the two words on the basis of their appearance and pronunciation to distinguish one from the other, discovering the different alphabets (and vowel signs) they are made up of in the process. She sees the alphabet 'र' (r) is common to both but the first alphabet (with the vowel sign) is different. She remembers all of them, building up a collection of alphabets in her mind.

(I would like to add an aside here. The child learning Hindi may take a slightly different path to learning the language than one learning English because Hindi is a phonetic language so it's generally easier to associate the alphabet with the sound (pronunciation), whereas English is less phonetic and more alphabetic. But I presume, the process of language acquisition would be broadly the same.)

Anyway, children develop a collection of alphabets which they discover and decode themselves on the basis of their appearance and pronunciation. These alphabets, and different oral language reference points and they use them to randomly guess and read unknown words. They enjoy doing this and every time they decode a new word they feel a sense of achievement. The momentum builds up, rapidly with the help of their peers and adults, increasing their collection of new words, new alphabets and reference points.

Children become readers, starting from a few sentences and without coming in to notice when they start reading whole stories. But here I would like to again point out that they usually read material that is meaningful to them. They start with short stories, may be it end fast and everything comes in front and without complications. But soon their thrust to read large text in simple sentences that is easy and uncomplicated. They progress to longer stories with more complicated sentences. But even when they begin reading more involved texts they still love shorter stories and poems.

Some observations

Children who learn to read in this way do not merely decode text but read with comprehension. A couple of children of the same age at ANDS had gone the alphabet route in other schools before joining us. We saw they read mechanically without comprehension, just stringing together the alphabets. They had to first unlearn many of the things they were taught and start afresh when they developed a desire to read. We see that children who are forced to learn to read take more time to read whereas those who learn by the ANDS method picks up reading much faster and also love to read. That shouldn't come as a surprise because every alphabet and every word is their own discovery, not an imposition.

As I have said earlier, they read what interests them – I haven't seen any child reading non-fiction or difficult articles at this early stage of reading, unless they have a context for reading such material.

And here's a recent observation of nine-year-olds discussing the caste system in a 'sense of history and society' learning session. One child in the group was from a traditionally deprived caste and had experienced caste discrimination in her life. She asked a question: What if a girl from a low caste married a boy from a high caste? How would their parents react and what should the couple do?. They all had some discussion on the topic in the classroom. The children knew each other and were able to connect with the question and topic. The discussion continued and led to three of the eight children reading a comic book "Bhimayan" on Dr Ambedkar's life, his struggle and his work to eradicate caste in our society, brought to them by the facilitator.

Writing

Children begin scribbling from the moment they learn to hold a crayon, pencil or piece of chalk. That's much before they come to school. My daughter got her first crayons when she was two years old and began scribbling randomly on paper or any surface she found. She felt excited when she saw the crayon left a mark so she continued scribbling. This helped her get a better grip on the crayon and she soon began drawing lines and curves.

One day she saw her random scribble was a half circle and she tried to complete the circle. That required a little more control of her hand movement (motor control). She did not succeed in her first attempt but got better and better as her hand became firmer. Playing with toys also helped her develop motor control. Her objective was not to gain motor control but to close a circle. Children begin drawing with random scribbles, then lines and circles, big and small, and then draw objects or human figures with features like mouth, eyes, hands etc. They keep trying to improve their drawing and add more detail.

As the drawings get more complex and detailed, children may get attracted to the textual world if their environment is rich in such material. They are excited when they write their first alphabet but it is a drawing for them. A sense of the importance of text usually comes after the age of three years. Just as body language is an important part of oral language, drawing plays a significant role in developing writing skills. I have seen three-year-old Khushi writing over the written text, which is among the initial explorations of text writing. Children later begin to copy words, their names in most cases, or words that are relevant to them. The writing is large and unformed but gets better as they develop confidence. They also begin remembering a few words and their pronunciation.

As they grow older, the next step is to attempt to write new words by shuffling the alphabets. They do not get distracted by *matras* (vowel signs) in Hindi or bother about them. For them it is a part of word-picture. But they do visualise the word is a combination of alphabets and *matras*. Later, they write new meaningful words. After this, they move on to two word sentences, then to bigger sentences, a paragraph and more. It's not a totally linear process, completing one step and moving to the next. But there is lots of back and forth; every next step helps them complete the previous stage. For example, they would still be learning to write new words when they are writing two word sentences.

Grammar and using the proper *matra* happens at a later age and takes more time. The text they write is meaningful. I have observed children begin with routine writing at ANDS– such as a greeting card or a letter or note to their parents/friends, or class experiences/reports. It could be because they get fewer opportunities to write stories and poems, although a few of them do make attempts in this direction. I think such writing comes at a later age, after they have developed their writing and language skills.

Practices at ANDS

Language is crucial to all learning. As outlined earlier, we have organized resources and activities to help the children develop their language skills at ANDS. Creating a language rich environment around children. Teacher and children together work and prepare the text and past it around and use it as and when possible are the best possible ways to motivate them for language acquisition. That's why we do not confine language exploration and learning to one room but extend it to the entire school campus. There is a special room for language to organize resources, provide specialised exposure and reflection but the entire campus is converted in a text-rich environment.

We also have informal spaces where children can chat with adults. There is no hierarchy or authority in any formal or informal space or conversation. This stress-free environment with richer contexts and reference points encourage children to experiment with sound and text to develop, by trial-and-error, all four language skills for communication and interaction.

Multilingual environment – We are proud to call ourselves a school with a multilingual environment. Most children know their home language and are comfortable speaking it but are also familiar with other languages, which include dialects, tribal languages and mixed languages. We treat all of them equally and they thrive in each other's company, each bringing their own quality and richness. In fact we welcome children communicating in other languages. In a multilingual class, it is imperative that every child's language is respected and becomes part of the facilitation strategies. So multilingualism is our identity. There is a positive relationship between multilingualism and cognitive growth, social tolerance, divergent thinking and scholastic achievement. During the morning music session we make available songs of different languages and dialects.

Room for Language & Enquiry

As we have mentioned earlier, the entire school is a resource for children's language exposure, but we also have a special 'Room for Language and Enquiry' that houses resource materials and facilitates/organizes the activities related to language learning.

The activities and resources to learn the four language skills (listening, speaking, reading and writing) includes library, baatcheet (informal discussions) on their experience and question, stories, poems, films, puppets and theatre.

There are posters in Hindi and English, some made by the children. Adults develop poem/poetry posters with children's drawings as a background. There are spaces for children to put up written texts. Words the children use or hear in stories and discussions fill soft boards and even the walls. The boards also display children's questions, their written work and their written creations. We have created a platform and activities to let them speak and listen to their peers and adults in their own style and language. The children express themselves freely both orally (speaking and listening) and in reading and writing. Children sit with the facilitators on a carpet spread in the room to listen to stories and participate in discussions. A couple of chairs and a table lie in a corner to use as required.

The textbook: In a conventional classroom of 25 students, all would have one book to study language known as textbook. This sounds little odd to me. What if each child has different books. Then the classroom would have 25 different books in a classroom. The Language room has a library of more than 2,000 Hindi and English books. We also keep sets of NCERT and other textbooks, workbooks developed by Eklavya and learning materials produced by groups working in innovative language education. The facilitator uses these as and when required.

We have seen children comfortably going through more than one textbook. During the summer vacation, Prakriti asked me for a book to read. She had just begun reading and I was reviewing an NCERT textbook at the time so I gave it to her. She finished going through the book in 4-5 days. Completing a textbook was never on our agenda, our focus being on the child's learning in the area of enquiry, with a textbook only being one of several means to achieve the objective. Fortunately, children were able to cover most of the NCERT content in this process, which has also been a demand of the parents.

Classroom activities

There are many examples available of best classroom practices. We have using organized and informal discussions and activities as classroom pedagogy for language learning. Let me give you a glimpse of a classroom activity reported by one of our facilitators, which I translated from our Akriti newsletter (issue 4)[3]:

> *The children, aged 4-to-5 years demanded I narrate a story in the language class. I had the NCERT textbook Rimjhim II with me. I selected the story 'Shekhibaz makkhi'. The children enjoyed the story. There was a dialogue in the story. The lion tells the house*

*fly, "Go away or else I'll kill you". I repeated
what the lion said, with a word changed: "Go
away or else I'll squash you". This led to the
children giving their own versions. Ananya
said, "Go away or else I'll make a sandwich of
you." Samrat said, "Go away or else I'll make
halwa of you." Then Suchi came up with, "Go
away or else I'll make a bulb out of you." The
children then started picking objects visible
in the room to make their own statements.
Finally, Jannat said, "Go away otherwise I'll
make papad of you." She used 'otherwise' in
place of 'else'. Shatakshi pointed out we can
use 'otherwise' in place of 'else'. The children
then began making sentences using 'otherwise'
and 'else'. Towards the end of the session they
decided to enact a drama of the story and they
performed it in front of the whole school,–
Anil (Language facilitator at ANDS}.*

Sustaining language and communication activities

Children employ a variety of ways to acquire language
skills. We provide them with ample verbal and non-verbal
opportunities for self-expression. Two such opportunities
that we have institutionalized at ANDS is the 'Podium' and
the wall paper "Ullu bullu bachche" to help them become
more comfortable with the written word.

Podium: This platform for oral expression is a one-hour activity set aside at the beginning of the school day for students and facilitators to sit together in a relaxed, informal setting to reflect and share their thoughts on what they did the day before. Each child is encouraged to speak to the group about how they see their experience of the previous day and convey the sense to the others. Any response the speakers get from the group helps them refine their narrative. The platform allows children to overcome their inhibitions in expressing themselves in a group setting. Having started out in Hindi, they are also encouraged to use English words, phrases and sentences.

Initially, the podium was an oral activity for children aged above 6 years but we later included younger children as well. The children seldom appear to listen attentively or sit still, especially the younger ones – at least that's what visitors tell us. But we have clear indications that they do listen carefully what the speakers are saying even if they are wandering around the room. They make pertinent comments about what's being said.

When we introduced the podium to younger children it was far more chaotic initially. Then we introduced group discussions but we couldn't sustain them for long. Then we tried mixed sessions with younger and older children but eventually switched back to the regular format of separate sessions. We maintain a podium report of all the children, noting down what they say. This data is important for assessing their progress through the academic year.

We now have three age-groups for the podium activity. The oldest group has learned to write so they write down what they want to say, exchanging their podium copy for some other student to read aloud. Sometimes the facilitator reads it. We never point out mistakes or correct them -the reports are read as they're written. It's good to see them laughing at their misspelled words, like one day a child wrote 'sutary' for 'story'. Everybody laughed, including the child.

Newspaper: motivation to read and write – One child, Bihu initiated a personal newsletter. This grew into an activity to encourage children to compile their own wall-paper. They decided, after much discussion, to call it 'Ullu bullu bachche'. It's a display board paper that brings together news, write-ups, pictures, art and other contributions 'filed' by our reader-reporters. We believe it's already begun to have a positive effect on children's familiarity with the written word. We hope it will develop as a platform for children to play and experiment with written language.

Concluding remark

Better learning is possible in a complete context that includes the family, school, society and environment. This is even more evident in the context of language learning. Unfortunately, our focus reduces to elements and outcomes that are quantitatively measurable, basically an examination of writing and decoding text. Logical analysis, comprehension, understanding co-relations and the world around, vocabulary, etc are a necessary part of language acquisition and come with it. But due to our mind-set we continue to focus on learning the alphabet, words, sentence construction and grammar. I do agree it's possible to mechanically learn a set of concepts or skills but these make more sense in a contextual setting. Like us, many other people working in the field of education are experimenting to develop child friendly and innovative pedagogical tools and techniques to make language learning a more holistic process but these efforts are mostly done in isolation.

Expecting the same results with the same 'treatment' from all children is unrealistic. Each child responds differently so it is difficult to predict what, how and when she learns. It is better to expose children to a range of activities in a holistic and democratic manner and let them learn on their own at their own pace. It then becomes unfair to measure their progress through a common examination. Assessments should run in parallel with the learning process so timely course corrections can be carried out in the process.

Exploring mathematics education at ANDS

Like in other areas, we moved away from conventional approaches to studying mathematics at ANDS.

There were interesting set of activities that makes mathematics education realistic. One of them was the idea of educational currency, which proved to be a strong tool for children to gain command over numbers and related concepts.

But first, allow me to share how we explored mathematics education at ANDS, beginning with why we think children should be introduced to the world of mathematics.

Minimum expectation: We use numbers and their operations in our daily life. So we would like children to recognise numbers and patterns in using numbers so they can make calculations that are useful in their daily life.

Exposure working with the abstract: We generalise and retain information in abstract form in many aspects of our life. I mean by abstract information i.e. representing anything using language or symbols.

I find that mathematics can be a useful tool for children to experience how to work logically with abstract information.

Analysing exhaustive possibilities: We work with abstract information/symbols and explore exhaustive possibilities within certain frame. This is one interesting aspect of mathematics as we work with abstract information in the form of symbols and have no limitation or other effecting elements to extend the possibilities. This allowed us to work exclusively on the basis of logic.

Let us take an example of shapes to understand this. If two lines connect we require introducing the concept of angles. All possible Angles can also be categorised in different ways like acute, obtuse or right angle.

If we use three line segments to form a closed construct we introduce the triangle, which can also be of three possible types determined by the angle –acute angle triangle, right angle triangle, obtuse angle triangle. No other triangle is possible. We can also categorize these triangles on the basis of their side ratios. If no lines are equal to the other we have a scalene triangle, if two lines are equal we have an isosceles triangle, and if all three lines are equal we have an equilateral triangle. No other triangle is possible in this frame. We have explored exhaustive possibilities logically in both the cases.

This is how we work with abstract information/ symbols and explore a range of possibilities within a certain frame. We have to consciously design methods and systems where children see exercises and mathematical concepts in realistic situations. Otherwise, working with symbols and axioms in isolation could alienate children from mathematics, which is a common phenomenon in conventional mathematics teaching. Allow me to point out what happens in conventional mathematics education.

Issues in mathematics education

Mathematics education needs to evolve a lot more than language education, where alternative, more holistic approaches are gaining currency, although the situation on the ground is still fairly pathetic. The basic issues which I talked about earlier in language education apply equally to mathematics education:

Narrow perspective: Mathematics is perceived largely as numbers and number operations in written form. Schools insist on working with algorithmic methods and we seem to be stuck there. Otherwise mathematics can be an excellent exercise to extract patterns, generalizations and make logical explorations with abstract concepts. This is again probably due to the pressure of having measurable outcomes that can be judged in examinations. I'm suggesting we should look beyond.

Elements in isolation: Schools focus their efforts on children learning numbers and their operations with shapes on paper and boards. We have little or no space for mental calculation, which we require in real life. We do not let children explore in realistic situations so mathematics becomes a 'dry' subject most children do not enjoy doing.

Linear design: Like with language learning, schools design a step-by-step progression in mathematics learning. This seems sensible because of the hierarchy of the content. The tentative sequence of teaching numbers in average schools would be up to 5 in the first year, up to 10 the next year, and up to 20 thereafter, with basic addition and subtraction, two-digit addition and subtraction and, later, multiplication and division.

The issues may be the same and even common to other subjects, but the treatment of these issues will differ from language to mathematics and this fact should be recognised in the pedagogical approach to learning mathematics:

- ✓ In language we can skip activities that focus on learning alphabets and learning them in isolation is not the best way forward. Children will still learn the alphabets if we adopt a methodology that has more comprehensive language learning outcomes. But Numbers in isolation have a meaning unlike alphabets. In mathematics, however, we have to keep narrower objectives in mind in designing activities with more comprehensive learning outcomes because understanding number value, for example, is necessary to move forward.
- ✓ We could start working in a realistic context and understand numbers in live and concrete situations but, at the same time, we must ensure the children

learn to work with abstract numbers without context as well.

✓ Mathematics is hierarchical so we need to have gradual progression, with each new concept helping children improve their understanding of previous concepts, although we do need to think more about the sequence as comprehensive design.

The nature of content and its hierarchy thus dictates that we adopt a different treatment in mathematics pedagogy. Comprehending content is a bit complex so I'll try to explain in simpler terms with little elaboration.

Mathematics content

The content is abstract so studying mathematics is analysing abstract information. I began the chapter discussing this abstraction and would now like to take some more space to talk about the term. 'Abstract' is a mental construction, a quality or process at the idea level that is separate from the object or event. In language, abstract is the opposite of concrete or particular. We use language to communicate and one aspect of language is that 'meaning' must be shared if we are to communicate. If we use the term 'windows' we understand the reference because we keep some absolute features that are common to windows in mind, although if we draw a window, it might differ from a drawing by someone else, because we may follow different specifications. So when we talk about the 'window' it is abstract but what comes on paper is particular.

Mathematics is also a language to communicate that uses abstract symbols and axioms.

I believe that these axioms must have emerged from real life situations and experiences. For example, if we see a tree or wall, we know that a tree or wall is more stable as these are perpendicular to the ground. These items suggest that things, are exactly vertical on the horizontal ground, steady for longer time compare to the one slanted. May be, based on this observation we defined this arrangement using the geometric lines as right angle, and even named it 'right angle'. This 'right angle' is a reference to define other angles. Bigger angles than this are 'obtuse' and smaller angles are 'acute'

But we must remember that although our study of mathematics can be linked to real life situations, the study itself remains at the abstract level of symbols and axioms. Any attempt to study them in any other way – say, by drawing a line in geometry – will be an approximation, a model, and not an absolute value. This is because a line by definition has zero thickness but a line drawn in geometry doesn't. Euclid expressed this well in defining a point in geometry – 'that which has no part', which essentially means it has no width, length or breadth, an indivisible location.

Working in the abstract makes mathematics very precise and absolute, with universal conclusions that brook no exceptions. When you work in the abstract with axioms and sub-axioms, you control every element that may affect the conclusion, so all exhaustive possibilities can be calculated and defined.

That's why accumulated mathematical knowledge does not change. We merely extend our knowledge when we seek to move to finer clarity, like when we move beyond Euclidian geometry to other dimensions.

As a subject, mathematics has a significant place in most areas of enquiry. It uses symbols and logical thinking to communicate ideas and concepts.

Journey of number content

In elementary education, the three major content areas studied in mathematics, are numbers, geometry and measurements. I will discuss content related to numbers to share the learning journey of a child. Number learning is a conceptually complex area of learning. The concepts and sub-concepts are interwoven so they may not follow the sequence given below but every new concept upgrades the understanding of previously learnt concepts.

I am interested to list and elaborate various basic concepts related to numbers before moving ahead in the section. As the understanding of wide dimension and nuance of number concepts would help us understand the level of complexity a child would be grappling with.

It would also illustrate various possible learning journey of Numbercontent which a child may be engaged with at any given point of time but unconsciously our method may exert pressure to teach in a sequence we find logical.

A child who can be said to have understood 'number' has essentially gained an understanding of all these concepts and sub-concepts.

Pre-number concepts:

There are a set of concepts children discover before starting to learn numbers, which we can call pre-number concepts.

1. **Senses of quantity** – Children hear sentences such as "Give me a black pencil" or "Give me three pencils". So they may initially perceive numbers as adjectives. Gradually, as they are exposed to different situations, they discover these words have something to do with 'quantity'. For example, Abeer, aged two years, started saying, *"Chhat"* (saath - seven) in response to the question "How many chapatis do you eat?" He was responding to "How many?" When he learnt to say 'ten' he randomly chose seven or ten to answer. It takes time for a child to comprehend that each number word refers to a specific, unique numerosity.

2. **The concept of 'oneness'**– After couple of months, Abeer started using one for 'one' and three, five or seven for 'more than one'. By the age of three years, children can use and understand 'one' and 'more than one'. They start exploring other places where the quantity 'one' can be used, such as chocolate, first, building, city, one o'clock and so on. The property of 'oneness' is not visible in any of these, unlike other properties such as colour or shape. It is an abstract concept that children grasp before entering school.

3. **Objects and their relationships** – The parallel journey of **matching** two objects also begins. Children start matching the two before they are three years old. Abeer would stand on a chair and say "I am uncha (tall)." He understood the characteristic 'height' could be different when comparing. Children figure out that characteristic differ and can be compared by looking at different objects -big/small, hot/cold, smooth/rough, tall/short, heavy/light. This leads to the concept of 'the same', which they use for **sorting** things. At ANDS we found young children enjoy sorting things by 'the same' properties. They join us when we sort jumbled blocks. They may begin sorting by colour before sorting by other attributes.

Matching leads to understanding the concept of **one-to-one correspondence**. When a child distributes chocolates to her friends, each child gets one chocolate and the child may find the number of chocolates is just right or maybe there are extra chocolates. She discovers 'quantity' as a property of a group.

Seriation and sequencing are foundational to our number system. Seriation is gradually arranging objects by size, length or height in increasing or decreasing order. Ordinal words (first, next, last) are used when giving children directions. The items are put in order so that they are counted once and only once. Putting items in order is a prerequisite to ordering numbers.

At ANDS we do a number of activities to strengthen these concepts. For example, children collect sticks and arrange them in ascending/descending order. Not all children aged 3-4 years can arrange them in order. Conceptually, they have understood tall/short while matching objects. But I guess activity with concrete materials may involve more sets of abilities or maybe arranging sticks is not of their interest or need. They find using these sticks more interesting so they are more inclined to learn, like if they have to build a house, they need to know whether a stick is too big or small for the roof etc.

Class inclusion and number conservation: The reference here is from Piaget. The understanding is more advanced than simple classification - that some classes or sets of objects are also sub-sets of a larger class. (For example, there is a class of objects called dogs. There is also a class called animals. But all dogs are also animals, so the class of animals includes dogs). Number conservation is the realisation that objects or sets of objects stay the same even when they are shifted around or made to look different.

Subitizing: The term can be defined as instant recognition of a number pattern without counting. The pattern can be reconstructed without knowing the amount.

- Finger patterns
- Dot patterns
- Other patterns (dominos)

Subitizing helps children see small collections as one unit. This provides an early perceptual basis for number, but it is not yet 'number knowledge'. They require exposure to various senses of number in addition to the above concepts to develop number knowledge.

Number knowledge:

Number sense – The term means 'an understanding of number'. "Number sense is sometimes defined as having good intuition about numbers and their relationships. It develops gradually as a result of exploring numbers, visualizing them in a variety of contexts, and relating them in ways that are not limited by traditional algorithms." This is a long journey of developing a hold on numbers so I'll expand on this aspect.

A parent of a six-year-old girl commented during her assessment that he did not find growth in her understanding of number. "Last year, you said she knows numbers up to 100 and this year, too, you say she understands numbers up to 100," he said. I used the same technique I used with other parents to explain what his daughter was doing during the year with numbers up to 100.

I begin with a question: "Do you feel some difference in your understanding of numbers up to 100 and your child understands of numbers up to 100?" They usually clearly differentiate: "We understand better than our child." "What is that difference?" would be my next question. "For example, would 27 have the same meaning for you and your daughter?" I point out this is not the case. "You have

147

comprehensively internalised the numbers. Your daughter is still developing her sense of number up to 100. Every day she gets exposed to different properties of numbers, which all add to her understanding of number," I say.

Let me give another argument to clarify my point. What are the differences between 10, 100, 1000? One may reply 10 has one zero, 100 has two zeroes, 1,000 has three zeroes. If I ask the same question to a child who has been running a 'vegetable' shop in market, he would probably reply, "You may get a small amount of green chillies for Rs10 and a week's vegetables for Rs100. But Rs1000 will get you enough vegetables for more than two months."

In our school children encounter the value of numbers in real life experiences that give them a better sense of number, not the 'dry' image of a symbol that gives little operating sense of what numbers are.

I do not see a unique sequence of achieving milestones in learning numbers but these milestones are all part of the process to develop number sense and understand the concept of number. The children start almost all aspects together, with exploration in one area helping them improve their understanding of previously explored areas.

Children come to school when they are three years old with an understanding of counting numbers up to five and the very soon learn to count to ten. We find Piaget and others have made observations that show a different development in children's understanding of Numbers.

Count all and count on stages: If asked to count additional objects (say 2 fingers) with a small number (say 4 fingers) children at a certain age will not count from 4 onwards (i.e. 5, 6) but will start counting from one. I have observed six-year-old children doing this. When you ask Apramay to add 4 (showing 4 fingers of one hand) with 3 (showing 3 fingers of the other hand), he counts all the fingers starting from one.

Cardinal number and ordinal number – Children aged 3-4 years get confused between understanding 'one' and 'first'. For example, if you ask them to pick the third object in a sequence of pebbles they may pick three pebbles.

Number conservation: Piaget observed that children get confused about quantity if you line up a collection of objects in two different lengths. Shiva, aged 3 ¼ years, would always say the number of pebbles were more if you lined them up in a longer row.

Number name, sequence and quantity: Children start using the number name in their mother tongue at a very early age. They start with one, two and three and say the initial numbers name and quantity by the early years at home. They may also start learning the number name in sequence in the school.

Children recite numbers they know in sequence. Five-year-old Samrat counted one, two, three, four, five, six, seven, eight, nine, ten, eleven, seventeen, eighteen as 'seeker' in a game of hide and seek. She had heard the numbers and knew the number name in sequence up to eleven after which she picked number names that were vaguely familiar. Initially children remember the sequence as rhymes. Gradually they start connecting number names with their symbols and combinations. Their grasp of number quantity evolves alongside but gets difficult as the quantity goes beyond a certain number. One needs to apply grouping or some other mechanism in order to count. Children begin with random grouping then move to groups of ten, which coincides with our number system.

I found children wrote 100060024 for 'one thousand six hundred twenty four' in a study I did (Maithil 2001). Number name has a different pattern than number symbols. Actually the number name does not follow the same place value logic. It follows a grouping of ten. So for every ten and multiple of ten we have to introduce a new word. There are small differences at various other places as well. For example, in Hindi and English the numbers up to 20 have separate names but Hindi has a little more complexity in not strictly following the system of group names beyond 20. For example, 29 is '*unthees*', which means 'one less than 30' whereas in English it is 29 twenty nine. This makes it a more complex system to understand at an early age so children memorise number names. Fortunately, the number names are used in daily life as well so they get many occasions to speak and listen, which help them remember the names, which can be called a stable number sense of a number.

Number symbol and its combinations: Children quickly observe and understand that there are only 10 symbols and all other numbers are a combination of these symbols.

However, they take time to get a sense that every possible combination stands for a unique value.

Pattern in written numbers: Numbers are arranged in ascending order and in groups of ten like an array, which shows that the combination of different symbols comes with a sequence -number relation with other numbers, smaller and greater than, number properties, even and odd numbers and so on

I recently printed a room-sized 'snakes and ladders' game that children can play on. It's a bit different from the conventional game. It starts from zero and the first line ends at nine. Only basic symbols (single digit numbers) are in first row. There is a small gully for the child to walk along. The number 10 comes just above 0 in the upper row. This way the numbers are reorganized to display their pattern. So 16 is just above 6 and so on. It helps the children understand symbol combinations, groups of 10, patterns and their relation with other numbers.

Number line: This is another suitable method to organize number, giving a lot of scope to understand the concept. It goes way beyond the basic number sequence and can be used in future to develop a deeper understanding of numbers. An organization has developed a tool similar to the number line, which we call number mala. I believe the mala is based on research carried out by the Freudenthal Institute, Nederland and other mathematics educators. The mala is a 100-colour bead string that has properties similar to the positive number line, with beads in different colours arranged in groups of 10. It is tied horizontally on a wall in our numeracy room. We have number tags that can be easily put on it. Let me relate an experience illustrating the strength of this tool.

I was taking a visitor around the numeracy room. I asked the children to show 48 on the number mala. The visitor put a tag on 48 and did not turn back to check as he was confident he had done it right but a child cross-checked several times. example: One day Ambar was counting one by one to put a tag on a number, but a few days later when she had less time to attach the tag, she used groupings of 10 on the same number mala. I was surprised and asked her about the change in approach after the class. She said, for her, there was less chance of making a mistake going one by one compared to groups of 10. It means she required more time to understand both methods are equally useful. In fact one can crosscheck using the other method.

Number sense is dynamic because it is layered. A child may spend a large amount of time to internalise different numbers while others may move ahead with a basic understanding.

Operation: Addition means merging while subtraction means taking away. These are the two main concepts of number operation that a child comes with to school. Exposure and opportunity to these operations in a more complex setting will help the child develop an entirely new level of number sense and meaning of numbers. Multiplication and division are next level concepts. Children start using these operations at a very early age but they go on to use these concepts in new and more complex situations (i.e with bigger numbers)once they gain a basic understanding of numbers.

They should explore mental calculation first, which is what they require most in real life situations compared to the algorithmic way. They come up with various possibilities of mental addition, which I've jotted down:

- Break up the numbers strategy – For example 57 + 38 might be calculated in this way: 57 + 30 is 87 and 8 more is 95
- Front-end (left to right) strategy – For example, 124 + 235 might be calculated in the following way: Three hundred (200 + 100), fifty (20+30) nine (4 + 5)
- Compatible number strategy – For example, to add 78 + 25 you might add 75 + 25 to make 100 and then add 3 to make 103
- Balancing strategy – For example, 68 + 57 becomes 70 + 55 (add 2 to 68 and take 2 from 57)
- Compensation strategy – For example, for the calculation 47 + 29, one may think (47 + 30) − 1

Place value: The concept of place value can be described in terms of a few other mathematical properties. I call them sub-concepts of place value because they can be seen as independent concepts. They require a different cognitive level to understand and show that learning place value is a continuous process.

Based on the place value concept, The number 1324 would be written: $\mathbf{1324 = 1 \times 10^3 + 3 \times 10^2 + 2 \times 10^1 + 4 \times 10^0}$, the symbols x and +, 10 and its power having a certain purpose in this expanded form. One cannot comprehend just by looking at it.

Let me put down what those sub-concepts are. Our decimal system is characterized by the following four mathematical properties. Let us take an example that we need to count thousands of coins and write the quantity for a bank.

- **Base-10 property:** The values of the positions increase in powers of 10 from right to left. We may count coins in groups of 2, 3, 5, 10 and so on. The decimal number system suggests counting in groups of 10.

- **Positional property:** The quantities represented by the individual digits are determined by the positions they hold in the whole numeral. Since the decimal number system has only 10 fixed symbols (0,1,2,3,4,5,6,7,8,9), counting the coins using symbols till 9 is easy as we have a unique symbol but in order to count beyond 9 we need to use other symbols or combinations of the existing symbols. These combinations have to have some logic to produce them. The place value system gives weightage to the position of these symbols.

  After exhausting all the numbers in sequence in the first position, which we call the 'unit' place, we place 1 at the second position which we call the '10s' place, as it is comes as the tenth number and conventionally is towards the left. The unit place is now again vacant to put all the numbers in sequence up to 19.

  At 20, we replace the 1 at the 10s place by the symbol 2. This pattern continues till we exhaust all possible combinations of symbols in these two positions. We extend to the third position when we reach 100 – the '100s' place. Again, after exhausting all combinations of three digits we move to next position, the'1000s' place.

That is how positionality works with number and we use 'power' to represent positional value, with 10^3 equal to 1000 (thousand), 10^2 equal to 100 (hundred), 10^1 equal to 10 (ten), 10^0 equal to 1 (unit).

- **Multiplicative property:** The value of an individual digit is found by multiplying the face value of the digit by the positional value. For example, in 1324, the positional value of 2 is 20, hence 2X10.
- **Additive property:** The quantity represented by the whole numeral is the sum of the values represented by the individual digits.

Schools teach place value by asking children to write the number in columnar form - units, 10s and so on - and then write the expanded form - 1234 = 1000+200+30+4. Simplifying the number in the name of its expanded form or externally imposing the '10s', '100s' place-based column may make the concept difficult for a child to understand.

I found class 6 children were confused using zeros to write any number. They wrote 100030024 for one thousand three hundred twenty four (1324), which seems sensible. They appear confused by numerical representation of numbers (Maithil 2010). I suggest that if children grow with numbers they definitely pick up different properties, like numbers grouped in 10, sense of positioning and so on, which makes it easier to comprehend place value.

There is much more to number, such as natural numbers, decimal numbers, fractions, rational numbers, irrational numbers, ratio, proportion, percentages, negative numbers etc which come with a better understanding of numbers. The list of number concept is huge. I have been talking of only those concepts and topics that a child in primary school deals with.

The purpose of writing about these concepts with anecdotes and observations is to help us visualize the highly complex process a child goes through to learn numbers. We usually miss this journey. Reaching from '1' to '2' and '3' is a huge jump when working with children. '9' to '10' is another big jump of a different nature. Children learn numbers from real life situations. At school we have tools and space to help them in this process by creating additional opportunities to use numbers differently.

Whole number Vs place value-based approach

In conventional schools, we start with numbers from 1 to 10, then up to 20 in the second step, then up to 100 and so on. Much later, we introduce addition then subtraction, multiplication and division. I give below some arguments/existing methodologies for number learning and mathematics. At ANDS we start with a couple of these and evolve further.

✓ Existing alternative methods
✓ Activities at ANDS

I call 'whole number vs place value'. What exactly is this debate?

Whole number approach: Numbers should be treated as whole numbers at early stage, which means the number 32 represents 32 objects and we should not get into 3 stands for 3 tens and 2 stands for 2 units in the number 32.

Children acquire the sense of single digits. Similarly, they should be encouraged to acquire the sense of other combinations of digits without breaking them into place values. Mathematics educators who lead this debate have suggested materials and methods to teach counting and addition. Some alternative methods include:

- Colour-coded 100 beads string - The ganit mala (Usha Menon, episteme1; and 'Children learn mathematics' by Frethental Institute, Nederland).
- Empty number line (Usha Menon, episteme1).
- Strategies of mental arithmetic (Constance Kamii and Linda Joseph); and 'Children learn mathematics' by Freudenthal Institute, Nederland)

Place value-based approach: The traditional approach to teaching the concept of place value is presently in school textbooks for the primary classes. Children are expected to learn to write the number in columns of 100s, 10s and units. I surmise the argument in support of teaching place value would be that the algorithms of addition, subtraction etc are the most efficient way to solve the sums. The understanding of place value is necessary to understand these algorithms, unless we want them to use these algorithms mechanically. A number of alternatives have been developed to communicate the concept of place value at the primary level.

- Matchsticks bundles or beads mala (Khushi Khushi, Class 2)
- Dienes block (Zoltan Paul Dienes 1950; and Khushi Khushi, Class 4)
- Pebble card (Khushi Khushi, Class 3)
- 'Snap, clap, tap' game (HBCSE mathematics textbook, Class 3)

I suggest the methods and materials used in the whole number approach can be used to begin teaching numbers to children since it is easy for them to relate the numbers with objects. The colour-coded beads string helps children start counting and they gradually catch the logic that the numbers are arranged in groups of 10.

In upper primary classes when a child's cognitive level is more developed, I suggest using materials recommended by the place value approach. These materials start with the grouping logic that children get a feel of in the whole number approach materials.

Understanding place value is a continuing process in children. It cannot be acquired in one go. The entire journey requires a good amount of time and experience of different forms of number to let them internalise these concepts. There is a clear hierarchy in maths concepts, with every higher order concept helping children to improve their understanding of previously learned concepts. But a hierarchical, linear progression with no realistic context just does not work in practice. It leads to disinterest and math phobia.

Realistic Mathematic Education (RME)

I would like to again refer to the context in which numbers exist. In teaching numbers in conventional schools, we extract the numbers from their context and teach them as number symbols, number names, number sequences and number quantity, working with algorithms to carry over/ borrow etc. Such extraction makes it difficult for a child to comprehend number fully.

Consider an example. A teacher asks a child, "If you have 6 chocolates and I take 4 of them how many are you left with?" The child may reply, "You are unfair."

What happens in this case? The child may look for an answer from a different perspective. We should not expect him to extract the numbers from the description and work mathematically to find the answer. We need to find ways to let them feel the number in a realistic context. This idea of realistic mathematic education (RME) comes from the Frethental Institute in the Netherlands. The term 'realistic' is not merely a connection with the real-world, but offers problem situations even in a classroom that children can visualise and be comfortable working in. So it is important to understand their personal interests before designing activities. I give a few examples from ANDS.

During our mathematics sessions, children have set up shops and other ventures to transact with ANDS educational currency. Parth offered a vehicle ride to earn money. It was an imaginary vehicle so the children lost interest after the first couple of rides. Parth was disappointed and came to me. I told him he needed to think of more realistic ideas that would actually interest his schoolmates. He switched his business and put up a game stall in which he arranged some items in a pyramid on a table and children had to knock the pyramid with a ball thrown from some distance. They paid for three balls and got double the money back if they knocked the pyramid down. The idea worked and he earned money.

It's easier to find a context to work with shapes and measurement. Children know shapes and can distinguish between them. The names of these shapes also help them differentiate. Let me share an classroom experience. I introduced children to different angles and asked them to look around to identify examples of these angles. One child said he had found a left angle instead of a right angle. I realized we usually show them an 'L' shaped angle to illustrate a right angle. If we limit the exposure to the shapes drawn by teacher it could be inadequate, as this child showed. So we should let children explore and find the meaning. They get to make finer distinctions between shapes and sub-constructs.

Take another example. We were studying the diameter of a circle. One child showed us a drainage cover with two handles exactly on the diameter to lift it. This was interesting. If the handles are fixed anywhere other than the diameter it is more difficult to lift the cover. The diameter divides the weight of the circular cover.

The idea of RME shaped our activities. We do not deal with number and other content outside a realistic context in math at ANDS.

Activities at ANDS

The room for numeracy and logic has its facilitator. My role is to interact with the facilitator to develop innovative methods together. I also used my spare time to conduct classes along with the facilitator. We did a number of activities with the children, which gave them the chance to explore various mathematical concepts and phenomena. Examples include working with the number mala, KBC (based on a TV reality show 'Who will become a millionaire'), working with educational currency of ANDS bank (children called it Shop-Shop), matchsticks bundles, board games, tangram puzzles, shapes, estimation, measurement etc. A couple of activities not in common practice are described below.

Educational currency of ANDS Bank: There is a board game called 'Business' in which players move along a pathway, buying cities and taking rent from others who land in these cities. I found this game presented a realistic situation that could help children learn math so I worked on developing a localised version, reducing the prices of cities to under 1000 and replacing the cities with the names of villages and cities in Madhya Pradesh. I tested the game when I was with Eklavya and got a good response from teachers and children.

I restarted working on the idea (without a board base) at ANDS, bringing in more diversity and different winning ends. We printed our own educational currency and, with many a ups and down, the facilitator managed to set up a shopping mall activity, with the children collecting empty wrappers and boxes to excitedly set up their market.

Initially 6-to-7 year-olds children couldn't differentiate between currency notes of different denominations. They used the money as tickets. We told them they could exchange ten 10 rupee notes for one 100 rupee note. They were more interested in collecting a larger number of notes. Gradually, they started differentiating between the notes, realizing 1000 rupees was more than 100 rupees. But the activity itself did not sustain for long and they lost interest, although collecting money and transacting were still appealing to them.

With a little discussion they started looking for other ventures to earn and spend their educational money. They came up with various ideas. One child opened a massage centre on a mattress, another started a puzzles and games zone. A couple of children made greeting cards for sale. We came up with the idea of an auction in which various school items and facilities are sold or charged for.

The activity extended outside the classroom to the whole school. Children require blank paper so paper was sold at the office table – Rs1 for a single side blank sheet, Rs2 for both sides blank sheet. One child responsible for games started charging for swings. Some children objected and called a meeting to rationalise the system, saying an auction is acceptable if every child gets the chance to earn from it. One child complained that other children were being allowed more time for the Rs10, which was charged for the games. Another exhausted all his money and asked for work to earn more. I suggested he make song posters for younger children. At times they kept money aside and worked out mutual exchanges. All these efforts were basically building up to work out a rationalised system for payments and services.

The children were keen to collect money but managing the money was an issue. We suggested setting up an ANDS bank for them to deposit their money every day, with the amount written on a notice board, but they wanted to keep their money. They then prepared a simple account book to maintain a daily record of their money while they kept their money in their pencil boxes.

This activity proved to be very productive, with the children developing different meanings and references about numbers.

We printed 1, 10, 100, 1000 and 10000 rupee notes, not 2, 5 or multiples of 5 because we wanted them to be exclusively exposed to groups of 10. Managing their daily account gave them the opportunity to add and subtract. They calculated whether the total amount had increased or decreased at the end of each day.

One day a child came to me asking for three sheets of blank paper. I said I would charge her Rs6 if both sides of the paper were blank. She gave me a Rs 1000 note. I asked her how much should I return. She said, "I don't know." I replied, "Then I can't give you the balance. I can also cheat you. So first calculate then tell me." She began mentally calculating. I prompted, "How many 100s are there." She told me to 'keep quiet'. Murmuring, "Ten notes of 100, nine are kept aside, one 100 note will have ten notes of 10, nine are kept aside, 10-6=4." Then loudly, "994 rupees." I happily returned Rs994. Every child experiences many such calculations every day.

We still have a long way to go to streamline the activity. But I would like to add the children also get exposed to concepts like percentages, profit, loss, interest and so on. The school should have spaces for such transactions with adults providing ideas or reviewing what's happening and only occasionally helping in the calculations, if needed.

Indigenous and traditional board games: We use many board/floor games for activities. One is the indigenous game changa astha, which is similar to ludo. It has a grid of 25 squares, four home bases and children move their counters to reach the centre. Players have four counter sat the home base. They toss dice to randomly generate numbers. If two dice are used they add numbers at every move. They plan their strategies – which counter to move when – developing logical thinking in the process.

Assessment system at ANDS

We attempted to create a resource hub at ANDS, changing the school design and educational pedagogy to let learners move to self-directed learning. We also attempted to develop an assessment system.

Let me begin by pointing out the dangerous consequences of the existing examination system. Let's first see how an examination is conducted. We ask children to write answers to some questions in a limited period of time. We may even conduct an oral examination where a few questions are answered on the spot.

The children receive a mark-sheet with grades for each subject. Looking at the mark-sheet does not tell us what a child knows, but it is an important document in our society. What if a child is in a disturbed state of mind just before the examination? The result would then declare he knows nothing about the subject, though he may actually be good in the subject. He could also be declared poor in the subject if his writing or expression is poor. The examination asks limited questions that cannot cover the entire syllabus. It's also a matter of chance whether it contains those questions the child is well prepared to answer.

The examination is perceived as a step in learning. Most students prepare intensely to get good marks but learning as an objective seems to be given the go-by. I remember an incident 6-7 years back involving a very young girl. She asked me to check what she had learned. She gave me her notebook and asked me to ask her questions from the book. I asked a question about rain. She could not answer till I used the same language for the question as what she had written. She then recited the entire half-page answer, even pointing out three places where she had corrected misspelled words. She could have given a much richer description of rain but no, she stuck to the prescribed answer. Her perception of 'examination' did not permit her to look for any other answer. This may seem an extreme example but the scenario is alarming.

The existing examination system divides children into categories of a few 'good achievers', with the rest being 'weak'. It acts as a filter. To use an analogy, you have many workers in a company but few achievers. Companies are designed that way – a hierarchy with a few people in leading positions and many at the base of the pyramid. The examination system has the same end result, producing a similar output.

I'm not the only one raising a voice against examinations. There are a lot of critiques available on the conventional system, with educationists coming up with reforms and alternatives. For example, In Eklvaya's education programme, the grading of questions and allocation of marks is reworked after analyzing a random sample of answer sheets. Children are allowed to take their notebooks to the examination hall and the questions attempt to gauge their understanding, for which they can freely use their notebooks. Many policy documents in education have also come up with progressive suggestions and recommendations.

The Kothari Commission Report (1966) states that *"the internal assessment or evaluation conducted by schools is of greater significance and should be given increasing importance. It should be comprehensive, evaluating all those aspects of students' growth that are measured by the external examination and also those personality traits, interests and attitudes which cannot be assessed by it." (9.84).*

The National Policy on Education (1986) also states that *"continuous and comprehensive evaluation should incorporate both scholastic and non-scholastic aspects of evaluation spread over the total span of instructional time."* (8.24(iii)).

The National Curriculum Framework - 2005 (NCF-05) proposes examination reforms in its position paper on 'Aims of Education', which says: *"School-based CCE system should be established to reduce stress on children, make evaluation comprehensive and regular; provide space for the teacher for creative teaching; provide a tool of diagnosis and remediation; produce learners with greater skills."*

The Right to Education Act (RTE – 2009) even says students up to Std VIII should not be made to appear for any board examination from the year 2010-2011, with *"a scheme of continuous comprehensive evaluation (CCE) to be implemented from Std I to VIII."*

According to me, CCE is a system of school-based evaluation of students that covers all aspects of a student's personality. It is an attempt to shift emphasis from mere testing to holistic learning. The word 'continuous' means evaluating a student's growth and development as a continuous process rather than an isolated event. It is built into the total teaching-learning process and spread over the entire academic session. The word 'comprehensive' means covering all aspects of the student's growth and development including scholastic, co-scholastic, emotional, physical, values etc. The word 'evaluation' could have several interpretations. I see its meaning as closely assessing where the student stands in any aspect of growth and development. This can suggest the direction for further inputs/interventions for holistic learning.

Need of assessment: I was clear there would be no examinations in ANDS. The RTE act is a strong base to support this argument. But we still need to know what are children growth pattern and development threads and what are the next level of activities we can initiate in a particular area of their learning. Parents are also curious to know how well their child is doing. These are valid and important concerns that have contributed to the development of our version of continuous comprehensive evaluation (CCE) for assessing the children's progress in learning.

ANDS idea of assessment: I have a simple understanding of assessment. If I need to assess the learning of a particular child, I will first collect samples of her work, organize them chronologically and review them as a whole. After that, I will be in a position to discuss her performance. It's not difficult for a facilitator to assess the changes she sees in a collection of drawings of a child done over the course of a year and comment on how her skills and aesthetics are developing. That's what we do, also pooling our observations and anecdotes along the way to keep track of the growth pattern of the child.

I'd like to give a point-wise picture of this assessment process, using the same example of a child's progress in drawing:

1. We compare her drawing with her own previous work in chronological steps, not with the drawings of other children. We are observing her growth exclusively.

2. We observe various parameters for assessing progress: her brush strokes have improved; the finish is better than the previous one; she has played with colours thus we get to know how her colour sense is developing or the changes are there in her aesthetics or we may discover the quality of her imagination; and so on.

3. The assessment is not limited to a few drawings or a fixed period but covers the whole year, providing a more realistic picture of how the child is progressing.

4. Drawing skills and aesthetics cannot be assessed by a written or oral examination; we need to assess the drawings skills.

5. We have not set a upper or lower criteria and the child can go to her optimum performance.

Sharing the assessment with parents:

When, we ended out first year, we decided to share our assessment with the parents. We had spent a year with their child so we wrote a 3-4 page note about her, covering all pertinent aspects, for which we had concrete evidence as well. There was no quantitative mark-sheet, just this personalized, qualitative note discussing how and what she had learnt during the year and the growth pattern in different areas - academics; co-scholastics; food, health and hygiene; attitude and temperament; social values; emotional growth. We also showed slides and videos of their child engaged in activities in school and showed them her creative efforts.

We had an hour-long chat with the parents about their child, asking them what they had discovered about her learning. We also gave them a two-page note about the inputs we had organized in different thematic rooms during the year. That was our formal assessment report, with the notes free of academic jargon and written in a language they were comfortable with. We did our level best to provide an accurate picture of their child's growth and development.

But we did realize we needed to be more organized at our end to collect the data, especially our daily observations of the children. We built up this system over the last two years and we see it evolving further as we mature as an organisation. We are a new and fairly small school but we feel such a system could be developed and implemented in bigger schools as well.

1. **Self-expression:** The students share their experiences of the previous day daily on the podium. This sharing enhances friendship and camaraderie among them, bringing greater joy and involvement in the day's activities.

The shared recollections serve two purposes - as a method of evaluation and to make course corrections. The students provide direct or indirect evidence of their progress while speaking and give honest feedback about the activities as well as their facilitators and peers.

This activity is useful in many ways but it is a time-consuming. The larger schools can develop a different version or make it periodic.

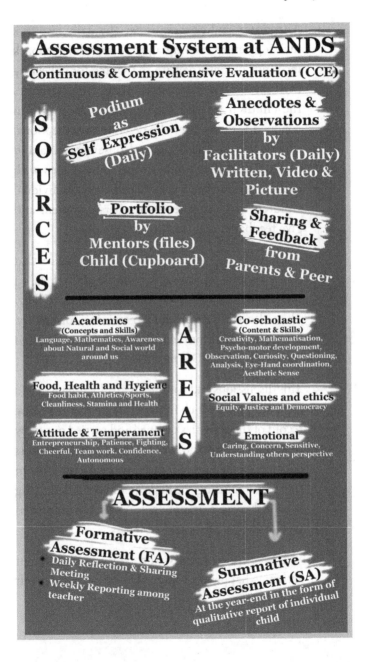

2. **Anecdotes and observations:** The daily feedback meetings every evening and the half-day feedback meetings on Saturday are the source for collecting this data. The facilitators share the activities the children do and the challenges they face in conducting them. They also describe any exceptional experiences or anecdotes and observations about children that may guide further interactions with them. They also track growth patterns of individual children. The other team-members comment and give feedback.

These meetings are an enriching experience that serves various purposes. We discuss and reflect on our experiences to improve our day-to-day practices. They also serve as on-the-job training for faculty. They are crucial for determining the direction and dimension of ANDS' progress.

This discussions and comments are documented in a feedback diary, which forms a valuable retrospective record of the activities planned and carried out every day, the performance of students and facilitators and the challenges that need to be focused on in future. Organising the huge quantum of data is big task and we are grappling to evolve an improved system for the purpose.

We take photographs and videos of different activities/happenings at ANDS to strengthen our database.

The facilitator used to maintain a daily diary in the first year but this couldn't be sustained due to lack of time. We need to see if we can start this process again.

3. **Portfolio**: This is the year-long collection of the children's creative output and work.

   a. **Personal cupboard:** Every child has a personal cupboard in which they keep their belongings including their art and craft work, and academic worksheets. Observations of how the cupboard is organized also contribute to the data for assessment.

   b. **Mentorship:** There is a mentor for every small group of children. The mentor has started collecting children's paper work in individual files. Older children (age 11-12 years) can be encouraged to maintain their own files.

4. **Parents and peers:** Feedback from parents and peers is another facet of comprehensive assessment of the children as well as a learning process for the school.

   Parents are stake-holders of the school. So we frequently interact with them to get feedback about their children and also share how their child has been doing in the school. We have prepared a comprehensive questionnaire as a checklist, with examples, for parents to express their feedback and observations in written form.

In the third year, the mentors made a mid-year visit to the children's homes to meet the parents and discuss the progress of their child. This has provided additional data about the children. In some cases, the older children also participated in these discussions.

Peers also play an important role in the assessment process of the children by sharing how their friends are doing and what are their difficult areas. A few incidents came to light during the podium and feedback meetings, which we incorporated in annual assessment report. This is one area where we need to think more about.

Areas of development

As a democratic school we do not impose a sequence of activities for children. We prepare a range of activities and motivating surroundings to let the child develop capabilities in different areas, acquire skills and choose his pace of learning. We can broadly divide the developmental data for assessment into three categories:

Measurable outcomes: Most of the academic learning outcomes are measurable. The facilitator's observations and worksheets help us assess a child's attainment level.

Non-measurable outcomes: The assessment of the outcomes is qualitative and based on the observation of facilitators, parents, peers and self. We have developed a format to register anecdotal observations of individual children.

Other changes and developments: Attitude and temperament, and changes in children's emotional state are registered periodically in the form of anecdotal observations of peers, parents, facilitators and self.

We have prepared a list of all possible areas of change in children for the assessment process. We may learn and understand more about these areas in future:

Academics (concepts and skills)

- Language readiness, language skills (listening, speaking, reading, writing), knowledge of home language along with Hindi and English, comprehension and world view, articulation and expression, literature and terminology.
- Pre-number concepts like sorting, grouping, one-to-one correspondence, seriation, classifying and order (of various characteristics like colour, shape, size, etc), sequence and pattern, number sense, counting, number, number operations, ratio, money, measurement, special understanding, data handling, algebra, geometry.
- Awareness about the natural and social world around us, self-awareness, concepts of sciences, exposure to scientific equipment and tools, confident use of computer.
- Awareness of art forms, brush strokes, colour, etc.
- Awareness of different indoor outdoor games and their rules.
- Contemporary issues in society, enquiry-based historical information, concepts of social sciences.

Co-scholastic (content and skills)

- Creativity, economy of thought, reflection, paraphrasing and summarising, sharing, communication.

- Mathematisation, mathematical modelling, analytical skill, logic, rational thinking, strategies for problem solving, planning and strategy, aims and goal setting, reasoning, estimation and approximation, psycho-motor development, maintaining validity, precision, accuracy throughout the creative process, generalization.

- Observation, curiosity, questioning, ability to hypothesise, exploration, investigation, experimentation, analysis, rigour, data representation, comparison, classification, pattern finding, eye-hand coordination.

- Motor skill, aesthetic sense, designing and visualizing, texture sense, order and beauty (aesthetics), brush stokes, cutting, pasting, expression, colour sense, sense of shape, form, size and ratio etc.

- Performance and healthy competition, sports spirit.

- Acting, cooperation and team work, repetitive movements, music, and rhythm, facing the audience, productivity and achievement.

- Referencing, questioning, critical thinking, decision-making.

Food, health and hygiene

- Food habits, athletics/sports, cleanliness, physical activities, flexibility and agility, stamina and health, physical activities, work experience .....

Attitude and temperament

- Persistency, straightforward, tolerance, daring, risk-taking, patience, fighting, arguing and negotiating with each other, cheerfulness, friendliness, optimism, independence, entrepreneurship, leadership, teamwork, rational and critical attitude, acceptance, confidence, productivity and achievement, co-ordination, leadership, helping each other, co-operation, autonomy.

Social values and ethics

- Equity, justice and democracy, honesty, respect and acceptance of other individuality (style of living, work, attitude, and interest and pace), objectivity, freedom.

Emotional

- Loving, caring, concern, sensitive, security, productivity and achievement, understanding others' perspective, personal biases.

Assessment of learning

The list of developments in children is huge. We have listed a few in order to create assessment indicators based on common understanding to keep track of our methodology and practice and make the environment worth living for children and us.

Formative assessment: During our feedback meetings, we share and discuss the changes we observe among the children as a group and as individuals. We trace the development threads and patterns of each child to understand the change and see what needs to be done to move forward. Below are examples of our formative assessment (FA):

During the classroom process (FA Level 1): One day I was conducting an EVS class with children aged 8-to-10 years. It was the monsoon season so we went out bug hunting. Amba declared she was scared of earthworms. Although she had no problems with earthworms the previous year, she said she did not like touching the wriggly creatures so she had no interest in the activity. However, the rest continued and returned to the theme room with earthworms in small boxes. They enjoyed watching them wriggling. Amba watched from a distance but I could see she was also enjoying the moment.

Veenu mischievously pushed the box of earthworms towards her. Amba reacted, taking a step back. Veenu then picked up the box and stepped close to Amba. The girl screamed and ran out of the room. An adult had to coax her to return after little while.

In most cases we do not interfere in such matters unless the children ask us to. But in this particular case, I intuitively felt I needed to do something, otherwise Amba would never get over her fear of earthworms. I firmly told her she would have to stay with the group and deal with the situation, do not run out. During the lunch break I talked to the two girls separately. I told Veenu what she did had only made Amba more scared of earthworms and said she should be more careful in future.

With Amba I reminded her she didn't have any problems exploring earthworms the previous year so what had made her change. She said they were '*gilgila*' (spongy) so she didn't like touching them. But our talk did make her realise earthworms are harmless and nothing to be scared of. The next day, she thanked me 'for removing my fear of earthworms'. I wondered how much the talk was helpful, but I made an assessment of what had happened and what could be the consequences. I would definitely call this a part of FA level 1.

After a series of observations (FA level 2): Five-year-old Prem usually avoided drawing. We came to know this in our feedback meetings so we observed his behaviour without letting him know. We also observed he loved playing games like cricket, stroking the ball with a maturity beyond his age. He appeared to attend the arts and craft sessions because of peer pressure. But he somehow coped. We shared our assessment with his parents, telling them he was not fond of drawing, just making circles and adding three marks for the eyes and mouth. That's all he did.

We found he could not tie his shoelaces despite having to do it daily. We felt there must be something we were missing but Prem himself said he would learn as he became older. But at the age of 6 years, he was having a tough time learning to write when other children in his group were progressing. We shared these experiences with his parents when they met his mentor. They also recalled that they always had to help him tie shoelaces. We requested them to take the matter seriously and look for toys and activities that could help him practice the fine and gross motor skills or take help from experts.

Even if these are not the best two examples of formative assessment, they do indicate the levels of such assessment. We observe a child's day-to-day functioning and collect some thread that needs to be considered and worked on further. In level 1 cases, it is an on-the-spot assessment that may require immediate response and action of the facilitator. In level 2 cases, there is a developmental issue involved so additional exposure and inputs are needed for the child's growth.

Summative assessment: At the year end, we compile the data to see the pattern of change in the child. Based on this we prepared a summative report and shared it with parents in personal meetings. The report has the following format:

1. Start with the striking features

2. Qualitatively elaborate the child's attitude and temperament as well as the emotional state and the change registered

3. Discuss the child's status in scholastics and co-scholastics – language, numeracy, EVS and science, music and dance, art and aesthetics, questioning, logic etc

4. Elaborate the child's physical health, hygiene and eating habits

Points 3 and 4 and sometimes a part of 2 are reported together since they are interconnected and cannot be dealt with separately. The report is a comparison with the child's previous status (the previous year or when she joined the school). It is free of jargon or statistics and written in a language the parents are comfortable with. Extracts from some reports are given below:

- *After a change in faculty, she developed a habit of not attending the numeracy and logic classes. In fact, she led the entire school to revolt against the facilitator. The school also supported her and discussed with the facilitator to make the classes meaningful for the students. The facilitator came up with an idea of the housie (tambola) game which pulled all the children back!*
- *Being a left handed person, she initially struggled a lot with the scissors while doing cut–paste activities (as scissors are manufactured for right-handed people). But she improved over the year as she is in a process of finding a way out. It is great to see her doing those activities today.*
- *There is a significant boost in his confidence. Initially, when he joined the school, he was seen as a shy and frightened boy. The extreme pressure to learn in a mainstream school had started destroying his*

self-confidence. We remember his second day when he was asked to bring something from a room. He went immediately, but when he realized he didn't know what he was supposed to bring, he began shivering. But the same child now spends time to understand everything whenever he decides to follow something through and expresses clearly if he is not interested in something. We congratulate and thank his parents for the support they gave him, along with our efforts. Our trust in him made his journey towards overcoming the struggles in a new environment smooth and helped him develop faith in himself and the school. Naturally, learning is now going to be fun for him. We are happy that at AND school we are able to provide an environment that gives space and time to children to feel comfortable and make a jump-start.

- *She also comes across as a truly sensitive and caring person, deeply concerned about everyone around her. This is her special quality that we observed over the year. To our surprise, one day when she came to know during a discussion that Bhagat Singh was punished with a death sentence which means to be hanged till death, she immediately said, "Didn't these Englishmen realize that Bhagat Singh must have been in pain?"*

- *His parents told us he is a slow learner. He is 12+ now and unable to cope with the cut-throat race in the mainstream school system. During his stay here, the school staff as well as his parents has seen a drastic change in his overall personality. Initially he used to find it hard to articulate the previous day's activities; he was even unable to form complete and comprehensive sentences. It gives us deep satisfaction that after a year, he is now able to narrate anecdotes with sentences in sequence and, sometimes, with some elaborations too. We feel that the inclusive environment of the school and the variety of stimulating activities practiced here have facilitated these developments in him.*

- *She had a habit of picking up things. Perhaps she is interested in collecting things and keeping them. However, since sometimes those things could belong to others, there was a need for her to understand that she either needs to ask before taking anything, or she could play with it and keep it back, or take it home with a promise to return. We are happy to note that there is now a change in her in this direction.*

- *She came to school with a few pre-requisites of language learning such as picture comprehension and recognition of some alphabets. In the Language and Enquiry room, she listens to stories very carefully and asks questions in between. Though her attention span is low now, she will improve according to age. Her language world-view was enriched in the school and now she has started articulating well with a punch line "Hai na!" She participates actively during discussions. She recognizes some Hindi and English alphabets and is now learning to write her name.*

- *She likes activities related to numbers. She is quite fast in them. She came with an understanding of some pre-number concepts such as sequencing, one-to-one correlation, etc and has reinforced those through school activities. She has a vocabulary of number names and their symbols up to 10 and is gradually improving her number sense with the activities she did in the school.*

Thinking and practice at ANDS

ANDS to me is a collection of ideas and practices. At times, the ideas have guided the practices and at times the practices have evolved into ideas. I'll try to share my learning journey of ideas and practices.

I derived my pedagogical approach to language education, mathematics education and assessment systems through my concrete experiences at ANDS. I would like to propose more elements of school design based on this experience and attempt a future projection of the ANDS idea in society. That image, I feel, is fairly moved from the idea of mainstream schools as we know them, with their framework of conventional practices and pedagogy.

Why school?

It's easier to talk about the 'how' of school than the 'why'. Schools are an integral part of society. Countries put in enormous resources to sustain and strengthen them, which imply they serve – or can serve - some important purpose in society. In ancient lore, princes went to gurukuls to learn the art of war, gaining proficiency in using weapons such as swords and bows, learning horse riding and so on. They also learned the scriptures, vedas, traditions and how to rule. They lived with their gurus, secluded from society.

This suggests that children of a certain class or identity had the privilege to acquire skills to play their prospective roles in society, develop an understanding of social behaviour and uphold their cultural identity. So schooling had three purposes – imparting knowledge, training in skills and preserving cultural identity.

These purposes remain relevant to this day. Modern society wants children to participate in the economic processes of tomorrow, for which they are sent to school to acquire relevant knowledge and learn the required skills. They also learn values and aspects of culture that help them fit seamlessly into their society.

Political processes which graduated and access to formal education becomes open for all citizens. This also meant that the responsibility to create such opportunities, institutions and their access becomes the responsibility of the state or the government. However it came with its own challenges of developing a model or a system for delivering education for masses.

I guess an idea of a school would have originated to address this challenge of delivering mass education. To have a commonality between what education the schools imparted the system of a common curriculum and textbooks was developed. This brought uniformity among schools.

In India, education is a subject under the jurisdiction of governments and we have a central body that formulates and continually upgrades educational content that is in tune with national considerations and contemporary needs. I believe a centrally designed syllabus and textbooks can never accommodate all possible interests and needs of a diverse country like India. The ideal way is to develop broad curriculum guidelines and let content and pedagogy be developed based on the regional context and local community needs.

The central body for formulating curriculum, conducting research and ensuring quality education is the National Council for Education Research and Training (NCERT). Its documents reflect the educational policies of the nation.

In 2005, the NCERT came up with a curriculum framework, called the National Curriculum Framework (NCF), that comprehensively details the 'why, 'what' and 'how' of education. NCF 2005 talks about all pertinent aspects of education in India.

My personal understanding of the ANDS practices are very much in line with the principles enunciated in the curriculum framework, so I would like to quote the relevant portions of this document that articulate my aspirations for children with more clarity than I feel I can achieve at this moment in time. I begin with a statement from the NCF 2005 Position papers (NFG on curriculum, syllabus and textbook, page-vii):

General aims of education

As proposed in the NCF 2005, the articulation of aims needs to serve two major purposes. Firstly, reflect collective socio-political aspirations of the whole society and secondly, serve a significant pedagogical purpose of providing direction to the teacher in choice of content and methods of education.

Aims can be stated in two parts as principles:

A. ***Values and ideals****: Education should promote in society, as well as help the learner develop, a rational commitment to:*

- ***Equality*** *– of status and opportunity.*
- ***Freedom*** *– of thought, expression, beliefs, faith and worship; as a value in life.*
- ***Autonomy of mind*** *– as independence of thinking, based on reason.*
- ***Autonomy of action*** *– freedom to choose, ability and freedom to decide and ability and freedom to act.*
- ***Care and respect for others*** *– going beyond respecting their freedom and autonomy, concern about well-being and sensitivity to all members of society.*
- ***Justice****: social, economic and political.*

B. Capabilities of individual human beings

- ***Knowledge base*** – *sufficiently broad knowledge base encompassing all crucial areas of socio-political life, and all basic ways of investigation and validation of knowledge.*
- ***Sensitivity to others*** – *Sensitivity to others well beings and feelings coupled with knowledge should form basis of rational commitment to values. 'Others' should include all life forms.*
- ***Rational/critical attitude*** – *Critical rationality is the only way to autonomy of thought and action.*
- ***Learning to learn*** – *the future needs of development of knowledge, reason, sensitivity and skills can't be determined in advance. Therefore, ability to learn as new needs arise in new situations is necessary to function autonomously in a democratic society.*
- ***Work and ability to participate in economic processes*** – *choices in life and ability to participate in the democratic processes depends on ability to contribute to the society in its various functions.*
- ***Aesthetic appreciation/creation*** – *appreciation of beauty and art forms is an integral part of human life.*

Our aspirations for children

Abraham Lincoln, a former president of the United States of America, once wrote a letter to his son's headmaster that narrates in a simple manner a father's aspirations for his child in school. It largely illustrates of our aspiration in simple language. I have taken the liberty of making changes in what

Mr Lincoln wrote to convey my personal understanding. For example, his words '*Teach him that for every scoundrel there is a hero*' become for me '*Narrate stories that for exploiters there are rebels as well*'. So here's my version of Mr Lincoln's letter:

> *I understand that my daughter has to learn that all humans are not true always. But narrate stories that for exploiters there are rebels as well; that for selfish politicians, there are dedicated leaders... share experiences with her that for rivals, there are friends as well. You could be one such rebel, one such leader and one such friend. Every human has both of these aspects and you have to choose your dominant inclination. Encourage her when she struggles to overcome her ego.*

> *I understand that it will take time to learn but discuss with her and let her experience the situations to understand that a little money earned is of far more value than a lot found... educate her to learn to lose and also to enjoy winning. Encourage her away from envy, if you can, educate about the secret of quiet laughter. Let her learn early that the bullies are the easiest to lick... Educate her, about the wonderful world of books... also let her experience of quiet time to ponder the eternal mystery of birds in the sky, bees in the sun, and flowers on a green hillside. It is good to work hard, not to defeat others but to win.*

In school, educate her that it is far more honourable to fail than to cheat... advocate to have faith in her own ideas, even if everyone tells her that she is wrong... educate her to be gentle with gentle people, and tough with the tough. Help her to develop the strength not to follow the crowd when everyone is getting on the bandwagon... Educate her to listen to all humans... but educate her also to filter from all she hears on a screen of her truth and rationale, and take the good that comes through.

Educate her, if you can, how to laugh when she is sad... Educate her that there is no shame in tears. Educate her to scoff at cynics and to beware of too much sweetness... Educate her to sell her brawn and brain to the highest bidders, but never to put a price tag on her heart and soul. Educate her to close her ears to a howling mob... and to stand and fight if she thinks she is right.

Treat her sensitively, but do not coddle her, because only the test of fire makes fine steel. Let her have the courage to be impatient... let her have the patience to be brave. Educate her always to have sublime faith in herself, because then she will always have sublime faith in mankind.

Now I would like to move on to the different elements and aspects of a school system, my ANDS experience being the reference point.

Curriculum and syllabus

I'd like to begin with a crucial element: a 'flexible time frame' for learning. At ANDS, we support our children to develop and learn skills and gain knowledge, like all mainstream schools. One crucial difference is the time frame. Learning at ANDS is a relaxed journey that unfolds according to the interests and pace of each individual child. We do not have landmarks that children must achieve by a specific age.

We started with no fixed syllabus to be implemented in a fixed time frame. My past experiences of working with children, teachers and content gave me strength to move ahead with no fixed set of activities for children either. I had no plan or series of activities designed. Teachers (we call them facilitators) have the liberty to develop their own content for the set of children they are engaging with. More important, the children also have a role to play in deciding the content and activity they want to engage in.

I had a broad understanding of academic learning outcomes by the end of the primary grades. Children should learn to read and write in their home language (Hindi) and English and understand numbers and their operations. I was also clear we would be working with language and numbers in realistic contexts and children would definitely excel in these outcomes. Therefore, formal and informal discussions and numerous stories were our content for language. Similarly, various games and alternative teaching-learning materials were our source for learning mathematics. For science, we started with making working models using junk material. In the process, children got acquainted with various aspects of science that they could correlate further as their pool of experience grew. For other academic areas, we just moved ahead with children's questions. ANDS also provides enough and equal opportunities for games and exposure to different arts, crafts and music.

We made some preparations, like designing the school as a text-rich environment. We started collecting and creating resources, filling the school with such materials. Everyday interactions with these resources and text make the children curious to learn. Our internal feedback meetings, which take place daily, help us fine-tune our methods and academic flow. The approach is action and reflection, informed by rigorous discussion. The discussions focus on different aspects: How are we moving in different areas (outlined in the earlier chapters)? What are the development threads visible in each child? Do we need to look at the activities and content to improve their interconnections and rhythm? These discussions help clarify our theoretical positions and improve or modify our learning activities to correspond with the children's pace of understanding.

We have no single textbook but a collection of resources for different areas of enquiry. Textbooks are just a small part of this vast pool of resources available to the children. I believe the content of a textbook is a limited resource for children to learn through enquiry. Let me share two experiences at ANDS: Seven-year-old Prakriti had learnt to read a couple of months back. During her summer holidays, she asked me for some books to read. I gave her a Grade I language textbook that children her age study throughout the year in school. She finished it in five days. Aprameya had an NCERT mathematics book at home and he chose to complete all the matching exercises first instead of following the sequence of chapters and exercises in the book.

We started including the NCERT textbooks among the learning resources in response to suggestions from parents but we consciously decided not to limit ourselves to these textbooks although we did use their texts in learning.

<u>An observation</u>: Children get more or less equal opportunity to work in all areas of enquiry and activity, academic and non-academic, so no child in school develops a hierarchical understanding of subjects. For them painting and writing are at same 'position' and they aspire to develop their skills in all the areas. I also observed that children are still not fixating their inclination in one or two areas but they are enjoying themselves in all the areas. My observations also suggest that children in general very soon come to conclusions like 'maths is not my cup of tea' or 'I may not be a music person' and so on. In ANDS however, children retain interest in all dimensions for little longer before arriving at such conclusions.

Some loud thinking

Traditionally, schools have set objectives and methods that seem more in line with factory production, where you have 'raw material', 'fixed time', 'defined processes' and 'uniform products'. I object strongly to such methods and approaches. But society, schools and parents have a mindset to 'prepare' children for a 'productive' life, hence schools meticulously plan their learning processes to fulfil this role. Authorities articulate rules and develop rewards and punishments to administer the system.

Learning outcomes: If we want to build a house, we first prepare a blueprint that shows what the house will look like, how many rooms it will have, what the colour of its walls will be and so on. We then collect the required material and begin constructing the house, finishing it in fixed time duration, the final product being an image of the blueprint. In this situation, we have a clear final product and a defined work method.

Now take a different example, lets say of a scientist. She, too, has an objective and designs a plan to achieve her goal. But if her observations from her experiments point the way to a different line of investigation than what she originally envisaged, she has to make course corrections in her plan. These modifications in her research path are the result of her observations and logical analysis. Sometimes, they may also lead her to a new discovery, her 'Eureka' moment.

Education is far more complex than the above two examples. It may have elements of both these examples. I believe it is rather an organic process. I see it as an organic process where we may start with a framework but we cannot expect the process to proceed in the way we plan. We cannot exactly predict - although we may have a broad idea - how long the process will take, or how the 'final product' will turn out to be. In education, we want some development to take place in other people but we have no way to predict or assure that these developments happen in the same way as we have thought of. Whatever data we gathered about learning processes that can either be categorised as "work with children" or "learning outcome" but we cannot establish a 'linear' cause and effect relationship.

But schools apply this cause-and-effect formula i.e if we perform a certain activity, it should give a measurable result, which is defined as the learning outcome. This approach ignores the totality of elements that actively feed into the process. Most significant is the child herself, her background, her past experiences, her state of mind at that moment, her relationship with other people around and many other factors we may know nothing of. A school has many children so we have a plethora of factors coming into play. It would be unrealistic to predict the end result of a learning activity in such a dynamic scenario.

That's why I believe all we should do is design an activity, let children do the activity, and monitor and assess the direction and dimensions of the activity, making needful changes as we go along. The change would be in the direction of our aspired outcomes but even these outcomes may not be exactly what we envisaged. We cannot predict a time-line for such an action-reflection process. So we should be comfortable with these limiting factors - uncertainty about the end result and flexible time-span. And let's not forget that these would vary from child to child and topic to topic.

This poses a big question mark on objective-driven practice and syllabus-based teaching, both important constituents of mainstream education. What we can then do is organize resources, create a productive environment and develop a support system on demand for the child. Whatever we design must be flexible and open-ended, giving enough breathing space for children to move ahead in any direction.

ANDS is full of resources that permit open-ended learning but also comply with parental aspirations for language learning, numeracy and social questions. I believe children are naturally curious and work with purpose to explore a desired area of enquiry on their own without outside interference, learning its different dimensions in a resource-rich environment.

Personal belief systems: I strongly feel experiences 'switch on' or 'switch off' our learning. For example, one of my friends once told me, "I just stop thinking when it comes to numbers." She dreaded mathematics. Most of us have similar stories about disliking some subject or other. It could be music, language, literature, accounts and so on. This is true of attitudes and belief systems as well - we have no clue of how or what the child will pick up or drop.

I believe children are born curious and explore everything around them. It is society that encourages or discourages them by giving conscious or unconscious inputs and signals. Unfortunately, we have no way of measuring this encouragement/discouragement. It varies from person to person and situation to situation.

Let me share an example. A teacher told me a child usually comes neat and tidy to school but then lies down in the sand pit. His parents always complained he comes home dirty, with sand in his clothes. I can only assume the parents constantly told him to be tidy – society keeps dinning such messages into us: tidy is 'good', untidy is 'not good'. The child must have felt this constant pressure from his parents, maybe even resenting it, and probably wanted to experience the opposite – of being untidy and dirty.

We have no such do's and don'ts at ANDS. We all have our belief systems but as a school we are not judgmental and do not value or devalue anything. Neatness is left to the child. There is no insistence on being organized even if we do not encourage disorganised behaviour. We are rather relaxed but sensitively observe and make children aware of the consequences of their every action. We trust them to develop attitudes and values. Even the older ones (9-10 years) learn or relearn values and attitudes through peer interaction in a democratic environment. They also learn to recognise and develop their inborn talents. They do not undervalue any specific area, with academics, craft and games having the same weightage.

Inherent qualities and values: Society instils values in children. They internalise the values of the community they are born and live in. Values such as equity, justice and democracy are reinforced when they begin looking more objectively at the social system they live in.

But when it comes to inherent qualities like curiosity, creativity and persistence we have seen that they are among the first casualties of societal pressure. The struggle is to ensure these qualities are preserved and reinforced in every child. But the expectations of society and institutions like school are far too high. Plus, they are over sensitive to success and failure. I believe if we scale down our expectations and are sensitive to children, interfering less in their journey of growing up, we can preserve these qualities.

I think this is easier to do and what society and school attempting required lots of energy, system, rules, management so on.

Some practices

Discipline Vs self discipline: One of the first questions visitors to ANDS ask when they come to know that children are not bound by rules and can choose what they want to do in school is: "What about discipline?" Another is: "How can you let children decide what they want to do in school? It will be utter chaos." And a third: "How do you ensure discipline then?"

Discipline is insisting that children obey their elders, stay in given limits, do not talk without permission, do everything on time, do what others tell them to do. That's what most parents have in mind when they ask these questions.

At ANDS, we use a different term to talk about how children conduct themselves - self-discipline. It means they decide their own boundaries and modes of functioning. We insist, and are firm at times, that they stick to the codes of discipline they have laid down. We are aware that school is where they experiment with and learn self-discipline, so it's always possible they miscalculate or overestimate. But they need to have strong reasons for breaking their own rules. For example, time commitment is one element of self-discipline. Children plan their school schedule and work according to it every day. If they need to make a change in their schedule they have to talk to everyone getting affected by change in their schedule, especially the facilitators and their peers.

We encourage them to first solve the problem that prompted them to seek a change rather than ignore or run away from it. For example, if they find an activity is not engaging enough they can always give feedback and work to improve it, or suggest changing the activity, without disturbing the daily schedule, which would have a chain reaction and other repercussions on the other groups.

Punishment Vs natural or logical consequences: In the three years of the ANDS functioning I haven't come across a child being punished and I don't think that can happen in future if we continue in the same fashion. Schools have a provision called 'punishment' for acts that the community or individuals finds inappropriate. Punishment is a tool to get children to follow the rules and accept authority. I feel authority and rules act as constraints in the learning process.

Consider the following. If you want to catch a bus that leaves by, say, 4 o'clock you need to reach the bus stop before 4 o'clock, else the bus will depart and you will miss it. This is a natural consequence of not being on time for the bus. At ANDS, if I come across a child not keeping her promises I will be sceptical about her promises the next time and communicate my distrust through my behaviour. However, I won't stop her from making promises. It is not my business to interfere in her making or breaking promises and commitments. I want to explain this subtle difference through an example.

There is a splash pool in the school that children love to jump in. We suggested doing so only towards the end of the school day so their clothes are dry when they do their activities during the school hours. They agreed. However, two children could not stop themselves and jumped into the pool during lunch time. The others brought this to our notice. The two met their facilitator and admitted they had broken their promise. The facilitator asked what should be done. The two talked the matter over and decided they would not have a dip in the pool that evening so they stood watching the others having fun.

This would qualify as a logical consequence of their act, especially since it was they themselves who decided their own 'punishment'. The act had an interesting sequel. After a while, one of the children in the pool asked the others and the facilitator to let the two join in. All agreed. Nobody thanked or blamed anybody; they all just had fun in the water together.

Success and failure: Success is not central to the effort children put in; the work is given the highest importance. In fact, success and failure are adult impositions. A result is influenced by many factors so we should not recognise or blame a single or few factors. We need to take all of them into account. Adults as authority pointing out mistakes imply a shortcoming in children's ability, which may lead to a dead end or divide them. The community of children gets to know what is lacking and fills in the gaps. Every process has small success stories at every step so equating success with the final result negates the possibility of enjoying each moment of success.

It is harmful to create competition for success and fear of failure. I've observed changing attitudes in children even in a running race. Young children love the running and look to their parents for appreciation. Older children look to see where their friends are, as if to gauge their speed. Even older children spread their hands and try to defeat the others. We need to de-emphasise the environment of defeating and competition all around instead promote enjoyment of work which leads towards excellence.

Every child is unique. We make sure none of us labels a child 'good' or 'bad'. I insist on not giving a tick mark for 'right' or 'wrong'. I don't want the child to do things for the sake of the marking but for the content and its quality. We need to find other ways of showing appreciation for the effort they put in, we may give a qualitative positive feedback.

Administration

In last three years, I have worked towards a less hierarchical, almost flat, administrative structure at ANDS. I hold the post of director but mostly to serve official purposes. There is no principal and no hierarchy among the faculty. Everybody chips in, whether it is sweeping the hall, spreading the carpet, conducting activities, playing with children, discussing informally with them, communicating officially with parents and government departments, etc. As the team and school grew, each of us began focusing on a specific role. Later we realised we needed an administration office so we put up a table and chair along with a cupboard in the main hall.

As people joined the faculty, I started academic work again and slowly distributed my official responsibilities. For example, I used to keep track of every detail of the school's income and expenditure. Vijay helped me maintain the accounts but gradually took over the responsibility, using computer accounting software. My residual responsibility was signing cheques and verifying expense vouchers. We also strengthened our faculty, with Varsha joining to initiate our thrust in music, an important part of the ANDS curriculum. We are well staffed at present in all academic areas - language, mathematics, social science, art and craft and, partially, EVS.

Present struggle – At the academic level, we designed an evolving system that children are happy with and learning achievements are beyond our expectations. However, we face a financial crisis and there is pressure to increase the number of children. I know the numbers will slowly grow, but the school team would like to hasten the process because we may not be able to sustain our existing financial support. With finances driving the agenda, the team is seriously considering a more rule-based, hierarchical system that goes against the spirit of ANDS. I am listing some of the issue below, along with my suggestions.

Roles and choices: We initially assessed the needs of the school and then looked for suitable persons to take up these responsibilities. It sometimes meant an existing faculty member took up a responsibility for which a suitable candidate was not available, even if unprepared to do so. I suggest we now adopt a process where we mutually choose responsibilities and the person who takes up a responsibility defines the task and develops new initiatives that add value. For example, I used to circulate a note sharing the activities going on in the school. When Varsha got involved, she converted the note into a quarterly newsletter and widened its scope. If a task remains after responsibilities are distributed, it could be taken up as a group task or left unattended. That way no one performs a task that they are not interested in or are not ready for. We must respect individual choice and inclination and design a system keeping individual strengths and weaknesses in mind.

Human and rules – ANDS is moving towards setting up rules to function. The concern here is not to lose focus of the human factor in the observance of rules. By their very nature, rules are rigid and authoritative. It is hard to develop rules that incorporate all styles of functioning so we must be ready for the fall out, which in some crucial cases could be to exclude the very kind of people we are looking for.

Rules in organizations are designed on the basis of a set of assumptions – that people may not be honest, that they need to be supervised. You end up with a hierarchy of supervisors. The organization is no longer flat but pyramidal, with authority filtering down the pyramid. Trust becomes a casualty.

The idea should be to have a bare minimum of isolated rules in a setting like a school. We can always talk and find solutions for individual problems and, over time, develop a system that respects the human presence. Systems can have rules with a flexibility to entertain individual concerns. It may consume time and energy but it can be done.

For example, when ANDS started we did not fix a daily time-table. We asked the children to suggest a daily plan. They developed a perception of what they wanted to do. At that age they cannot comprehend time span but we still divided the day into periods that were flexible, either shortened if content was uninteresting or completed quickly, or lengthened if content needed more time. There was no timing imposed on them. I expect children need less time divisions as they grow older and learn to allot time according to their needs.

Concluding note

To conclude, I would like to stress that there is a strong need to re-think education and schools. Educationist John Holt has raised a deeper question in his book 'How children fail?'

> *"Intelligence is a mystery. We hear it said that most people never develop more than a very small part of their latent intellectual capacity. Probably not; but why not? Most of us have our engines running at about 10% of their power. Why not more? And how do some people manage to keep revved up to 20% or 30% of their full power – or even more? What turns the power off, or keep it from ever being turned on?"*

This was written way back in 1964 but our schools still work with learning outcomes in a fixed time frame. This unbearable stress in schools kills children's creativity. Educationists have even flirted with the idea of disestablishing schools. As Ivan Illich says in his book 'De-schooling society':

> *"The pupil is 'schooled' to confuse teaching with learning, grade advancement with education, a diploma with competence, and fluency with the ability to say something new. His imagination is 'schooled' to accept service in place of value. Medical treatment is mistaken for health care, social work for the improvement of community life, police protection for safety, military poise for national security, the rat race for productive work."*

Existing schools are not producing what is expected. The present book is not merely a narrative of the learning experiences at ANDS. It raises a question: Why is there only a single type of school that prepares children for future, which is a euphemism for job opportunities?

What about being a social animal, interpersonal relationships, belief systems, etc. There are avenues but no institution has the status schools have. Will the future see more institutions gaining equal status in society? The vision is to have many types of schools that run with different orientations and aspirations, schools with a theme-based design that give a stake to the children and independence to the teacher.

Parents should have clear and multifarious options for their child to choose from, whether it is a conventional school offering instruction-based, result oriented learning or a democratic school or any other.

I have shared ANDS' evolutionary journey keeping this in mind. I have also given specific details of language and mathematics education and discussed assessment process, a crucial element of education that determines how to start a school with a difference.

What I propose for schools

I question the assumption that we can fully understand the learning process at a cognitive level. 'Teaching' is not possible, only 'learning' happens. The learning journey may not trace the same trajectory for all children. But there is scope to organize activities so learning happens with groups of children.

I propose that we focus on activities with multifarious possibilities for open-ended and free exploration. They include 'Podium' for language, 'ANDS Bank' for mathematics, and 'Question Box', an emerging activity, for science, in which children put up their questions and look for answers. These three activities have no end product in mind but they develop in sync with the child's abilities. We have to think of such activities and resources including textbooks that can help children explore further and develop their abilities. We have to move away from the textbook and syllabus-based approach to the open-ended activities approach.

We have to scale down our expectations and be sensitive to the needs of children, intervening only on demand. Our intervention should be to share our perception of possible outcomes and consequences or to help the child to move to the next level.

We require holding back our understanding of 'right' and 'wrong'. This is a difficult task because our beliefs, values and behavior are conditioned by the system we live in. Let the child choose for herself what is important and how important.

An important note

A lot is being communicated through non-verbal communication which is guided by personal values and belief systems. So you need to share among children and adults what your understanding as an institute is.

More importance should be given to the human element. 'Trust' children. At ANDS, flexible arrival time, timetable planning by children, free use of tools, minimum rules, every rule open to question at any point of time are some of the examples of trust in children. I believe this trust should be extended to adults in the school.

Natural Learning Model

At the end of the book I would like to reiterate that **children are creative and have an unfathomable capacity to learn. The agency of children needs to be recognized significantly in their education. We need to trust the child and develop activities/ material and processes to move according to children's interest and pace.**

ANDS was an experiment of this kind. We created ANDS as a resource hub with thematic rooms, decision-making platform, a comprehensive assessment system and academic activities such as Podium, ANDS bank, etc. We had aspirations about our children but did not design a rout map of the learning output and have got remarkable results.

I believe the ANDS experiment is a kind of proof of the theory which needs to spread across the education world. I call it the **"Natural Learning Model"** and personify it with the symbol given below for easy communication.

To draw this symbol I have placed uniform squares at different angles. A perfect circle automatically emerges in the center. We need to focus on the squares, which have equal sides and angles. In the same way, all the aspects should be given equal weightage in the teaching- learning process. Over-emphasizing any one aspect would disturb the final outcomes. This is what happens in the conventional mode of education where the child has no say in his/her education resulting in skewed outcomes.

I believe the remarkable change in the children's oral language was a result of the Podium activity discussed in the previous chapter. While developing the activity I had no clue about the result we got but had a belief that this activity would become a good platform for children to play with oral language.

Reference materials

I have reviewed various materials throughout the Journey and sometime referred these while writing the book. I cannot claim that I have understood the documents thoroughly but these do give useful linkages between theories and practices. I am listing down some of the materials below.

1. National Curriculum Framework (NCF) 2005; Executive summary of teaching of Indian language

2. NCF 2005 and its focus group position papers (January 12, 2015) – http://www.ncert.nic.in/rightside/links/focus_group.html

3. http://linguistlist.org/ask-ling/lang-acq.cfm#processdated August 29, 2014

4. Akriti newsletter, Issue IV - September 2014, Anand Niketan Democratic School (ANDS)

5. Right to Education Act 2009 (on 12 January 2015)- http://mhrd.gov.in/rte

6. www.arvindguptatoys.com/arvindgupta/**Danger** schoo.pdf

7. http://aleph0.clarku.edu/~djoyce/java/elements/bookI/defI1.html on 18 Sept 2014

8. http://www.learningandteaching.info/learning/piaget.htm#ixzz3PpFUkTWK on 25 Jan 2015

9. www.ictm.org/journal/index.php/imt/article/download/72/82 on 25 Jan 2015

10. http://episteme4.hbcse.tifr.res.in/proceedings/strand-iii-curriculum-and-pedagogical-studies-in-stme/strand-iii-curriculum-and-pedagogical-studies-in-stme on 25 Jan 2015

11. http://www.fi.uu.nl/en/rme/ on 25 Jan 2015

12. Eklavya (2002). Khushi Khushi grades 1 to 5– Primary textbook cum workbook for Prathmik Shiksha Karyakram (PRASHIKA). www.eklavya.in

13. Various documents about HSTP (Eklavya) http://www.cisl.columbia.edu/grads/presi/EKLAVYA/

14. HBCSE. (2001) Mathematics textbook of class 3. Mumbai: Homi Bhabha Centre for Science Education.

15. Zoltan, P. D. (1950). The multibased blocks. http://www.zoltandienes.com/wp-content/uploads/2010/05/ what_is_a_base.pdf (Retrieved on 13 sep 2010).

16. Menon, U. (2004). The teaching of place value –Cognitive considerations. In Proceedings of epiSTEME-1, India. http://www.hbcse.tifr.res.in/episteme/episteme-1/themes/math_edu_rsh

17. Heuvel-Panhuizen, M.V.D., Buys, K., & Treffers, A. (Eds.). (2001). Children learn mathematic — A learning-teaching trajectory with intermediate attainment targets for calculation with whole numbers in primary school. The Netherlands: Sense Publishers.

18. IGNOU AMT. (2001a). Teachers of primary school mathematics - Aspect of teaching Mathematics. New Delhi: IGNOU. IGNOU LMT. (2001b). Approach to learning 1 by IGNOU school of science. New Delhi: IGNOU.

19. Kamii, C., & Joseph, L. (2010). Teaching place value and double column addition. Artihmetic Teacher, 35(6), 48-52. http://www.learningnet-india.org/articles/tpvdca.php (Retrieved on 13 Sep 2010).

Printed in the United States
By Bookmasters